THE
FOOD &
COMPANY
COOK BOOK

Home cooking from the heart

THE FOOD & COMPANY COOK BOOK

©2021 Margaret Brough, Joan Gate &
Meze Publishing Limited

First edition printed in 2021 in the UK

ISBN: 978-1-910863-82-4

Thank you to Melvyn Bragg, the
Lakeland Dialect Society, the Spedding
family, Nick Shill, The Old Crown at
Hesket Newmarket and for the love,
support and patience from our families.

Written by: Margaret Brough, Joan Gate
& Katie Fisher

Edited by: Phil Turner

Photography by: Tim Green

Designed by: Paul Cocker

PR: Emma Toogood/Lizzy Capps

Contributors: Lucy Anderson,
Suki Broad, Michael Johnson,
Alexander McCann, Lizzie Morton

Printed and bound in the UK by
Bell & Bain Ltd, Glasgow

Published by Meze Publishing Limited

Unit 1b, 2 Kelham Square

Kelham Riverside

Sheffield S3 8SD

Web: www.mezepublishing.co.uk

Telephone: 0114 275 7709

Email: info@mezepublishing.co.uk

FOREWORD

BY MELVYN BRAGG

This book, like the Lake District out of which it comes, is in a class of its own.

Thirty years ago I finally put a roof on the barn next to our cottage in the far Northern Fells. The pigsties became bedrooms. The barn itself – quite a big space – proved to be perfect for parties. We started to hold them every Christmas, and in between whenever we could find an excuse. Scrums might be a better word to describe them. Fifty or sixty people turned up: neighbours from our hamlet, old friends from Wigton, new friends of all shapes and sizes from across the Lake District. Artists, teachers, labourers, lawyers, even politicians and ennobled persons made up a festival of Cumbria which starred one thing: the food. Before we decide on any event these days, the question is "will Margaret and Joan be free?" If they're not available, the event has to be rearranged. As Mrs Thatcher once said: "There is no alternative!"

Margaret and Joan are sisters from a farm just a few miles across the Northern Fells from where I live. Their catering comes out of a wide knowledge of local food and the infinite variety of local produce. Their company has become a big hit and a wonderful feature at many occasions and locations, from castles and houses of various shapes and sizes to barns.

Even on the wildest nights, with snow on the ground and frost on the way, people would heave across the county for these occasions, knowing that there would be a feast at the end of their journey. Sometimes their way was blocked by trees blown down across the road. One Christmas I accidentally set the chimney on fire and the fire brigade eventually arrived in full gear to put it out, then stayed for the party.

But the centrepiece was always the enthusiastic trail from barn to kitchen and back again for course after course of this great variety of food. Even as I write, I can taste the flavours of Penrith Peppered Lamb; Baked Venison Sausages with Braised Red Cabbage; Pheasant Pâté and Cumberland Sauce; Turkey Filo Pie; Spiced Beef and Cranberry Relish; Tipsy Apricots; Sozzled Sultanas; Baked Blueberry Cheesecake; Damson Ice Cream… on the list could go, dish after dish from scores of nibbles to scores of desserts, helped down by wine (foreign I'm afraid) and beer (from local breweries, of course).

And it's not only the food itself. They lay it out in royal style, and that gives the event a special feeling; you could call it love at first sight. There always seems to be enough for second helpings and even when the guests have departed into the black Christmas night, wrapped up outside and centrally heated, there's enough for a few days of grazing for the family as they talk over the events of the evening. These would include rolling back the carpets at the end of the night and dancing to the best pop music of our time.

By then, Margaret and Joan would have set off up and down twisting lanes, past the small ill-lit village where John Peel kept his hounds and rode into hunting legend, across a vast barren moor where ponies still run wild, and back to their homeland in Caldbeck (meaning cold stream).

Margaret and Joan and their friends have made Cumbria a merrier, happier and more contented place. When we're invited to parties around the north of the county, the final and clinching words are always "Margaret and Joan will be laying on the food."

Oh, and how could I forget the Solway Shrimp Tarts…

CONTENTS

OUR JOURNEY UP TO NOW

BY MARGARET BROUGH & JOAN GATE

We're sisters and farmers' daughters who developed a fascination with food as we grew up surrounded by excellent local produce in Cumbria, where we've lived and worked all our lives. There's seven years between us, with our brother Edwin in the middle, who still farms Park Head, our childhood home, with his family. As children, we had what you might call a countryfied life which revolved around the kitchen table. The farming day consisted of hard work broken up with breakfast, ten o' clocks, dinner (that's lunch to most people), teatime, then supper and a bite before bed.

Our memories of food include milk churns being collected from the farm; a travelling grocer who drove around the rural villages in his van, which even had a countertop bacon slicer; and a weekly visit on Fridays by the local butcher from Caldbeck, when the Sunday roast was often purchased. Mum would also visit the village shop with her basket and her little notebook. This old-fashioned way of shopping meant we always ate locally produced food, not forgetting our own lamb and Christmas poultry, which was reared on the farm. Tuesdays were always baking days, when Mum turned out plenty of cakes and bakes from the old AGA, using the farm's eggs and milk.

Betty and Edwin, our parents, were also great hosts who shared a love of good parties and good food. The house was often full of friends who came over for meals and games of whist, so it was always a happy place. One of the highlights for us as children was picnics in the hayfield, complete with Mum's homemade elderflower champagne. Once hay-time was over, we often travelled the 20 miles to the Solway coast for our holidays, though Dad always had to go back to the farm to milk the cows each morning and night. Dad's favourite time of all was Christmas, and also when we all gathered together around the table for birthday suppers.

We spent lots of time outdoors in the beautiful Cumbrian countryside too. Margaret's love of flowers began there; she would pick wildflowers from the hedgerows as you could back then, which she displayed in jam jars on the kitchen windowsill. The family farm, Park Head, is perched on top of a hillside called Warnell Fell which has gorgeous views over the Solway and overlooks the two villages of Caldbeck and Hesket Newmarket, and beyond to High Pike and Carrock Fell. We didn't know it then, but this childhood playground would also become the backdrop for pretty much the whole of our lives and careers to date.

Farmers' daughters often went into banking, became farm secretaries, or joined a catering course after school (unless you stayed home and worked on the farm) so that was an easy choice for us! We both took catering and management courses at Carlisle College, though not at the same time, where we learnt classic cookery alongside business skills. Our time there was very enjoyable and stood us in good stead for the future, although we actually began our careers in the school meals service.

They were great times in many ways, particularly because we didn't need to work weekends or holidays so there were plenty of opportunities to temporarily leave the hills behind and socialise in the city. Our hearts always brought us home though and we loved being members of Caldbeck Young Farmers, a wonderful youth organisation that gave us so many opportunities and taught us all sorts of life skills, from flower arranging and cooking on gas stoves to stock judging and public speaking, even changing a car tyre. The YFC was also something like a dating agency and is where we met our future husbands, Richard and Ian.

Meanwhile, our jobs as supply supervisors took us all over the county, so day-to-day life was very varied and made you think on the hoof. Not only was this a great grounding, and something that taught us how to work really effectively within a team, it also gave us our first introduction to outside catering. As part of a special team, we would cater for civic events and many grand ceremonial occasions that gave us a taste of the posher side of life. We cooked all sorts of things that we'd never heard of before, such as chilled lemon and almond soup, which took us outside the box and broadened our culinary horizons. From there we both went on to work at Higham Hall, an education centre near Bassenthwaite Lake run by the local authority that offered teacher training and weekend courses.

The housekeeping and catering teams that we had joined at Higham looked after every aspect of the guests' experience during their stays, including the fine dining which had an excellent reputation in Cumbria. The standard of the food there was indeed second to none; we learnt so much about seasonal cookery too, and had the chance to try out new dishes. Each of these steps in our careers so far had helped our progression towards the business we would soon set up together.

Margaret married Richard in 1981 and moved to a small farm called Matthew Rudding, half a mile from Park Head. In 1989 Joan and Ian were married at Caldbeck church, as Richard and Margaret had done before them. During these years we were always cooking in one way or another and in 1991, we decided to establish JM Caterers. Now that we had children - Thomas and James for Margaret, Sarah and Sally for Joan - working weekends instead of during the week was more suitable. We renovated a hay barn at Matthew Rudding into a catering kitchen, store and office which became our permanent base. We didn't seem to have any trouble finding clients, as we'd been networking without realising it all along.

Business usually found us by word of mouth and came in the form of anything from simple lunches and village hall dos to corporate events and marquee weddings. We often worked just down the road at Hutton-in-the Forest and remember with fondness the corporate suppers held in the walled garden for the Shakespeare summer productions. We bought a refrigerated trailer to make for an easier life, which we were great at driving but hopeless at reversing… though any bumps and scrapes were caused by our husbands, honest! The trend moved from cold buffets to complex hot meals which we mastered during many memorable events in the Great Hall at Naworth Castle, Brampton.

Sadly in 2001 this venue was brought to its knees because of the foot and mouth outbreak. The Cumbrian countryside was closed and the farming community was hit hard, with many farms losing entire herds of cattle and flocks of sheep. The only surviving animals from Richard's family farm were a group of in-calf heifers kept at Matthew Rudding. As the year progressed, the heifers calved and Margaret made gallons of surplus milk into butter and damson ice cream. She did this until the milk could be collected and sold to the dairy once more; friends, family and neighbours all enjoyed the produce in the meantime.

Marquee weddings were our mainstay at this point, and we had built up a good reputation as caterers with a well-known presence in the area: people remembered us. We had a great team who loved to help out at events and became our second family; there was lots of fun, laughter and many more stories for another time! We were also passionate about using lots of local produce, and tried to reflect the time of year in our food, which was where the company tagline of 'a taste for all seasons' came from. So JM Caterers was doing well enough, but our children were older now and more independent, and it seemed like a good point in time to move in a new direction, and to have our weekends back again!

Food & Company began in 2005 with a desire to do cookery demonstrations, something Margaret in particular had always wanted to try. We travelled to London and did a bit of market research; it was clear that the general public were becoming more interested in food, and with all our experience in the catering and hospitality industry we decided we could do it.   Mirehouse, a historic manor and home to the Spedding family, had a garden hall in an exquisite setting looking out over Bassenthwaite Lake, not far from our homes. It seemed like an ideal place to hold these events, so we transformed the space into a homely but stylish demonstration venue and kitchen area.

The first year of our new venture was really quite exciting; we bought some great cookware, crockery, workstations and equipment to give the demonstrations real professionalism. The idea was to offer people a real food experience; they didn't need to get hands-on but they did get to taste everything we made. We ran a fairly small programme of themed demonstrations initially but thankfully, it proved very popular and we've been very fortunate to have lots of return customers over the years.

Sadly, we never got started again after our winter break in 2019, because the national lockdown in March 2020 meant everything was cancelled for the rest of that year. Of course, there have been positives to come out of this forced quiet period… not least this very book! We had no idea how to make a book happen but clients were always asking if we could produce one, since we regularly gave out recipe sheets at our demonstrations. We hope this compilation meets those expectations, and although we haven't quite decided what our next step will be, our book marks a celebration of the last 30 years, and we are proud to share our food and our company with you in these pages.

MORNING COFFEE, TEATIME TREATS

We've always baked as mums and farmer's wives, so this chapter is important to us because it's full of delicious sweet treats that you can enjoy from morning to teatime. At Food & Company we are well known for the warm welcome we offer to all our guests. Once you walk through the arched doorway at Mirehouse, saunter along the covered veranda and emerge into the garden hall, you can leave all the hustle and bustle of daily life behind. Fresh coffee is served in gorgeous blue mugs from the former Wetheriggs pottery, alongside a tempting selection of homemade biscuits and traybakes. This really sets the scene for a friendly home-from-home vibe that puts everyone at ease.

Many of our hints and tips on these recipes have come from our participation in the Hesket Newmarket Agricultural Show, a local event that has always been a huge part of our family traditions. Every September you will find us setting out our baking entries in the industrial tent along with dozens of local people, all hoping to win a prize ticket. As children, we were always encouraged by our parents to enter the show and they even donated a trophy for the junior section. Betty and Edwin would have been immensely proud that their great-grandchildren, Jessica, Charlotte and Evie, are now baking for the show too.

We hold our own annual event in the garden hall which is inspired by the show called The Great British Tea Party, featuring afternoon teas served on vintage china that's been passed down through our families. Guests are invited to enter our baking classes and Margaret's sister-in-law Gillian awards a 'Best in Show' and runner-up for each of the four classes. Gillian is a renowned home baker and judge on the show scene, and always generously shares her tips and advice for showing.

We hope that you can recreate those feelings of welcome and community with your own home bakes for family and friends. Great cakes start with good quality ingredients; we always use free-range eggs, butter for the best flavour and unwaxed lemons when the recipe calls for zest. We still share fond memories with our children of enjoying Grandma's Shortbread with pan coffee (milky coffee) on the AGA, and we hope these tried and tested recipes help you to create some treasured family times in the kitchen too.

"Best in Show"

ALMOND SLICE

A favourite morning coffee treat amongst our Food & Co family, this traybake has a crusty top sprinkled with toasted almonds and a gooey filling which is naturally gluten-free.

Preparation time: 25 minutes | Cooking time: 30 minutes | Makes 24

INGREDIENTS

250g plain flour

60g caster sugar

Pinch of salt

150g block margarine or butter

1 egg yolk, beaten

4 tablespoons apricot jam

120g caster sugar

120g icing sugar

120g ground almonds

60g ground rice

2 eggs

30g flaked almonds

METHOD

First, make the sweet pastry which is sufficient to line two trays. You can freeze the spare half for another time if it isn't required.

Sift the flour, sugar and salt into a large bowl. Cut the butter into small cubes and add to the flour mixture. Using your fingertips, rub the butter into the flour until the mixture resembles breadcrumbs. Add the egg yolk and mix until a pliable dough is achieved. If time allows, let the pastry relax in the fridge to prevent shrinkage.

Preheat the oven to 180°c. On a lightly floured surface, roll out the pastry thinly into a rectangle large enough to line an 18 by 28cm Swiss roll tray. Spread the apricot jam evenly over the uncooked pastry base and set to one side while the filling is prepared.

Sift both of the sugars into a bowl and add the ground almonds along with the ground rice. Stir well to incorporate everything together. Break the eggs into a small bowl and beat lightly with a fork, then add to the dry ingredients and mix thoroughly. Carefully put spoonfuls of this mixture over the jam and spread out to cover the whole base. Scatter over the flaked almonds before baking in the preheated oven for about 30 minutes or until golden in colour.

Cool in the tin before cutting into pieces and storing in an airtight container.

HINTS & TIPS

Substitute the plain flour with a gluten-free option to make this suitable for coeliacs.
The almond slices freeze well once cut.

CHOCOLATE BROWNIES

A simple recipe that children will love to make. This delicious, fudgy and lighter version of the classic brownie is versatile enough to serve warm with cream and fresh berries as a fabulous dessert, or simply wrap for an on-the-go treat.

Preparation time: 15 minutes | Cooking time: 40 minutes | Makes 15

INGREDIENTS

250g butter

180g dark chocolate
(54% cocoa solids)

150g caster sugar

150g light brown sugar

75g self-raising flour

4 eggs

60g chocolate chips

METHOD

Preheat the oven to 160°c and line an 18 by 28cm Swiss roll tin with baking paper.

Cut the butter into evenly-sized cubes and put them into a pan. Begin to melt the butter over a gentle heat.

Break the chocolate into small pieces, add to the butter and stir until almost melted. Remove the pan from the heat and continue to stir until the mixture is smooth.

Put both sugars into a large bowl and mix thoroughly to ensure there are no hard lumps. Sift the flour into the sugar and blend them together.

Add the sugar and flour mixture to the melted chocolate and mix well. Break the eggs into a bowl and beat with a fork, then pour them into the chocolate mixture in one go and mix to a glossy smooth batter.

Scrape the mixture into the prepared tin and sprinkle the chocolate chips over the surface. Bake on the middle shelf of the preheated oven for 40 minutes.

Leave the brownies to cool to room temperature and then cut into squares. Enjoy.

HINTS & TIPS
Use gluten-free flour to make a successful coeliac-friendly version.
Load the brownie with sweets and chocolates to create an indulgent edible gift.
These brownies freeze well once cut.

DROPPED SCONES & CUMBERLAND RUM BUTTER

A nostalgic store cupboard recipe which can be made in no time at all. We have great childhood memories of scoffing Mum's dropped scones as quickly as she could make them. The rum butter was traditionally served at christenings, where the empty bowl was handed around afterwards to be filled with silver coins for good fortune.

Preparation time: 15 minutes | Cooking time: 15 minutes | Makes 22 scones and 400g of rum butter

INGREDIENTS

For the scones

180g plain flour

60g caster sugar

1 level teaspoon cream of tartar

1 level teaspoon bicarbonate of soda

Pinch of salt

1 egg

150ml milk

For the rum butter

180g butter, cubed

240g soft dark brown sugar

2 tablespoons dark rum

Grated nutmeg, to finish

METHOD

For the scones

Sift all the dry ingredients into a bowl together. Break the egg into a cup, add it to the bowl along with most of the milk and beat well using a balloon whisk. Add more milk until you have a moderately stiff batter which drops off the whisk.

Using a piece of kitchen roll, grease a moderately hot griddle and then drop dessert spoonfuls of the mixture onto it. Once bubbles have appeared on the top, use a palette knife to turn the scones over. They should be uniform in colour. Cook briefly on the second side and when done, if you're not eating the scones straight away, lay them on a wire rack inside a tea towel. Grease the griddle in between batches and repeat until all the mixture is used up. For a professional look, use a piping bag to make evenly-sized scones.

For the rum butter

Very gently melt the butter in a pan on the stove, taking care not to overheat it. To ensure your mixture has a smooth texture, roll the sugar between two sheets of baking paper to eliminate any lumps, then place the brown sugar into a large bowl. Add the rum and stir so the sugar begins to dissolve slightly and absorb the flavours.

Add the melted butter to the sugar and rum mixture, then beat well with a wooden spoon until blended and smooth. Pour into a suitable china bowl and add a grating of nutmeg before allowing the rum butter to set. Cover and store in the fridge until needed.

HINTS & TIPS

Margaret cooks these directly on the slow AGA plate but they are just as successful cooked on a flat griddle. The dropped scones can be served with ordinary butter instead of the rum butter if preferred. Small lidded containers and dishes containing Cumberland rum butter can make lovely gifts for friends, especially at Christmas.

LEMON DRIZZLE

The queen of lemon drizzle is our lovely friend Sandra, who cheers everyone up with a parcel of this delicious light sponge and its sugary lemon crust. Simple to make, this is our take on the all-time family favourite.

Preparation time: 15 minutes | Cooking time: 30 minutes | Makes 16 squares

INGREDIENTS

120g soft margarine

120g caster sugar

2 eggs

120g self-raising flour

1 level teaspoon baking powder

1 large lemon, zested and juiced

90g granulated sugar

METHOD

Preheat the oven to 165°c and line a 23 by 23cm square tin with baking paper. In a large bowl cream the margarine and sugar together until light and creamy in texture. Break the eggs into a small bowl, lightly beat with a fork and then add gradually to the creamed mixture until thoroughly incorporated. Sift and fold in the flour and baking powder, then add the lemon zest. Mix the batter swiftly before scraping into the prepared tin. Bake in the preheated oven for 30 minutes or until the sponge is golden brown.

While the sponge is baking, prepare the lemon syrup by mixing the granulated sugar with the lemon juice until it forms a syrup. Use a pastry brush to gently brush the syrup over the top of the hot sponge until all of it has soaked in. As the cake cools, the topping will become crunchy and have a wonderful fragrant lemon flavour.

Once cool, store in an airtight container and serve in squares as required or freeze for later.

HINTS & TIPS

When in season, a lovely idea is to add some chopped fresh lemon verbena leaves to the sponge mixture.

FRUIT SCONES

There is nothing nicer than the aroma of a freshly baked scone filling the kitchen. This is the basis for a good sweet scone. Use your imagination to create something unique by replacing the dried fruit with something that you enjoy.

Preparation time: 10 minutes | Cooking time: 8-10 minutes | Makes 6-8

INGREDIENTS

240g self-raising flour (we use Carrs)

1 heaped tablespoon caster sugar

Pinch of salt

½ teaspoon baking powder

30g butter

30g lard

30g currants or sultanas

150ml milk

METHOD

Preheat the oven to 200°c. Sift the flour into a large bowl then add the caster sugar, salt and baking powder and mix them together well. Cut the butter and lard into evenly-sized pieces, add them to the flour mixture and use your fingertips to rub them together until the mixture resembles breadcrumbs. Stir in the dried fruit.

Add most of the milk and use a round-bladed table knife to mix the ingredients together, then gradually add the rest of the milk until a soft dough is formed. Turn onto a lightly floured board and, using a rolling pin or your hands, gently press out the dough to a thickness of 2cm. Cut the scones out with a 7cm fluted cutter, placing them onto a baking tray. You can brush the tops with some extra milk, but be careful that it does not run down the sides.

Bake in the preheated oven for about 8 to 10 minutes or until the scones are light golden in colour. Cool on a wire rack. The scones freeze well; for best results refresh from frozen in a hot oven for about 5 minutes. If using a 6cm fluted cutter, this recipe will make 10 to 12 scones.

HINTS & TIPS

Use a fluted cutter for sweet scones and a plain cutter for savoury scones.

GRANDMA'S SHORTBREAD BISCUITS & SHORTBREAD TRAYBAKE WITH GINGER ICING

A great family recipe handed down from mother to daughter, generation after generation. Nothing tastes as good as these light and buttery biscuits, with their unmistakable pinched corners and fork marks just like Grandma always made.

Preparation time: 15 minutes | Cooking time: 40 minutes | Makes 20 biscuits and 1 traybake

INGREDIENTS

For the shortbread

280g soft butter

150g caster sugar

360g plain flour

For the ginger icing

60g butter

3 teaspoons golden syrup

2 level teaspoons ground ginger

60g icing sugar

Sliced crystallised ginger, to decorate

METHOD

For the shortbread

Preheat the oven to 160°c. Cream the butter and sugar together until light and fluffy. Mix in the flour until a dough is formed and then turn out onto a floured board.

Handling the dough lightly, shape it into an oblong and cut it into two equal pieces. Roll out one half into an oblong about 20 by 15cm of even thickness, then cut into 20 squares.

Place the squares onto a greased or lined baking tray, leaving a little space between each biscuit to allow them to spread. Using your thumb and first finger, pinch the corners of each and then prick each one with a fork.

Bake on the centre shelf of the oven for about 30 to 40 minutes; the shortbread should be just beginning to turn golden in colour when done. Remove the shortbread from the oven and while it's still on the baking tray, dust with some caster sugar. Transfer to a wire rack to let them cool before storing in an airtight tin.

To make the traybake

Grease an 18 by 28cm Swiss roll tin. Roll out the remaining shortbread on a lightly floured surface and press it into a rectangle the same size as the prepared tin. Press the dough into the tin evenly and prick all over with a fork. Bake in the preheated oven for about 30 minutes, until a pale golden colour. This could be cooked at the same time as the shortbread pieces.

For the ginger icing

Make the icing as the shortbread traybake comes out of the oven. Melt the butter, syrup and ground ginger together in a pan, then sift in the icing sugar. Mix well until smooth, then pour the icing over the cooked shortbread. Decorate the traybake with the crystallized ginger pieces, then leave it to set and cool. Cut into small fingers and store in an airtight tin.

PARSNIP & WALNUT TEA BREAD

A reliable recipe for something a little bit different. The addition of parsnips makes
a moist and fragrant tea bread that keeps extremely well. Great for when you've got
all the family dropping in for a cup of tea and a catch up.

Preparation time: 15 minutes | Cooking time: 1 hour | Makes 1 loaf

INGREDIENTS

150ml vegetable oil

150g light brown sugar

2 eggs

1 small banana (approx. 120g)

180g self-raising flour

1 teaspoon baking powder

½ teaspoon mixed spice

60g walnut pieces

120g peeled and grated parsnip

½ orange, zested

1 tablespoon orange juice

2 heaped tablespoons icing sugar

10ml orange juice or water

METHOD

Preheat the oven to 150°c and line a 1kg loaf tin with baking paper. Using an electric whisk or food mixer, whisk the oil, sugar and eggs together until the mixture is creamy. Peel and mash the banana and add it to the bowl. Use a spoon to mix it in thoroughly.

Sift the flour and fold into the mixture along with the baking powder and mixed spice, followed by the walnuts, grated parsnip, orange zest and orange juice. Take care to mix and incorporate all of the ingredients thoroughly.

Pour the mixture into the prepared tin and bake on the middle shelf of the preheated oven for about 50 minutes. Check that the tea bread has risen and cooked through by inserting a skewer into the centre of the loaf and ensuring it comes out clean. If undercooked, return to the oven for a further 10 minutes. Allow to cool in the tin.

If you want to add icing, mix the icing sugar with the orange juice until smooth. When the tea bread has cooled, remove from the tin and peel away the baking paper before drizzling with the icing. Serve in slices, with or without butter.

HINTS & TIPS

Try substituting the walnuts with pecans or stem ginger.
This loaf freezes well.

PEANUT CARAMEL BARS

An Australian recipe handed down by a lovely local gentleman was the inspiration for this delicious modern traybake. These sweet treats are a great addition to a children's lunch box.

Preparation time: 10 minutes | Cooking time: 30 minutes | Makes 12

INGREDIENTS

For the base

180g plain flour

120g caster sugar

30g custard powder

¼ teaspoon salt

120g block margarine, cubed

1 teaspoon vanilla extract

1 egg yolk

For the topping

100g soft brown sugar

1 level tablespoon golden syrup

90g butter

120g blanched peanuts, roughly chopped

METHOD

For the base

Preheat the oven to 160°c and line an 18 by 28cm Swiss roll tin with baking paper. Sift all the dry ingredients into a large bowl and using your fingertips, rub in the margarine until the mixture resembles breadcrumbs. Add the vanilla extract and the egg yolk and mix until the mixture becomes a firm dough. Press the dough into the prepared tray and bake in the preheated oven for 25 minutes or until it turns golden brown.

For the topping

While the base is cooking, measure out the ingredients for the topping and begin cooking about 5 minutes before the base is ready. Put the brown sugar, syrup and butter into a saucepan, slowly bring to boil and then cook gently for no more than 5 minutes. Stir in the chopped nuts and carefully pour the topping over the cooked base, then spread it out evenly.

Return the traybake to the oven to bake for a further 5 minutes, then remove and allow it to cool in the tin. Once cool, cut into 12 bars and store in an airtight container.

HINTS & TIPS

If preferred, you can substitute the peanuts with almonds.

STICKY GINGERBREAD

There are plenty of good recipes for gingerbread in Cumbria, but this one is a favourite. Handed down from Joan's godmother, this is our go-to recipe for a sticky, moist gingerbread. The cook's privilege is to cut a corner piece of gingerbread from the tin and enjoy it while still warm.

Preparation time: 10 minutes | Cooking time: 40 minutes | Makes 16 squares

INGREDIENTS

120g block margarine

1 tablespoon golden syrup

2 level tablespoons treacle

240g caster sugar

300ml milk

1 heaped teaspoon bicarbonate of soda

300g plain flour

1½ teaspoons ground ginger

Pinch of salt

1 egg

METHOD

Preheat the oven to 140°c and line a 23 by 23cm square tin with baking paper. Gently melt the margarine, syrup, treacle and sugar in a saucepan together and once melted, remove from the heat and stir in the milk. Add the bicarbonate of soda and stir well to dissolve.

Sift the flour, ginger and salt together in a bowl. Add the melted sugar mixture and mix thoroughly using a balloon whisk. Break the egg into a cup and then add to the mixture, stirring well to ensure there are no pockets of flour left. Your batter should be smooth and lump-free.

Pour into the prepared tin and bake on the middle shelf of the preheated oven for 40 minutes. Ensure the sponge is cooked through by inserting a skewer into the centre of the gingerbread and ensuring it comes out clean. Cool in the tin, then cut into 16 squares. Store in an airtight container.

HINTS & TIPS

Best eaten the next day when a delicious sticky top develops.
Serve warm with custard for a traditional pudding.

EASY LEMON MERINGUE PIE

Making this sweet treat on a regular plate makes this such an easy recipe with no chance of the pastry shrinking or edges collapsing. A delicious citrus filling and soft meringue tinged with golden peaks make this a firm old-fashioned favourite, perfect for an afternoon tea.

Preparation time: 45 minutes | Cooking time: 40-45 minutes | Serves 8

INGREDIENTS

For the sweet pastry

250g plain flour

60g caster sugar

Pinch of salt

150g block margarine or butter

1 egg yolk

For the filling

250ml cold milk

150g caster sugar

30g cornflour

2 eggs, separated

60g butter, cut into small cubes

1 large lemon, zested and juiced, plus 1 extra tablespoon lemon juice

For the meringue

100g caster sugar

METHOD

For the sweet pastry

Sift the flour, sugar and salt into a large bowl. Cut the butter into small cubes and add to the flour mixture. Using your fingertips, rub the butter into the flour until the mixture resembles breadcrumbs. Add the egg yolk and mix until a pliable dough is achieved. If time allows, let the pastry relax in the fridge to prevent shrinkage, then preheat the oven to 180°c.

On a lightly floured surface, roll out half of the pastry into a circle large enough to cover a 25cm ovenproof plate. Trim the overhanging edges away. Bake the pastry uncovered in the preheated oven for about 12 minutes until golden. Remove from the oven and cool before adding the filling. Reduce the oven temperature to 160°c in readiness to brown the meringue. While the pastry is cooking, make the filling.

For the filling

Put the milk, sugar, cornflour and egg yolks into a small saucepan and whisk to mix thoroughly. Add the cubes of butter along with the lemon zest and juice. Stir the mixture continuously over a medium heat until it has thickened and the cornflour has cooked out. Once the mixture has boiled, pour carefully onto the cooked pastry base. Set to one side while you make the meringue.

For the meringue

Using a spotlessly clean bowl and an electric handheld whisk, whisk the egg whites until they are stiff and dry in appearance. Gradually add the caster sugar while you continue whisking until the mixture is thick and glossy. Carefully spoon the meringue onto the lemon filling. Smooth the edges first, then the centre and use the back of a spoon to make peaks on the meringue.

Finally, sprinkle the meringue with a little extra sugar and bake in the oven for about 10 minutes until golden in colour. Serve once the pie has cooled.

HINTS & TIPS

This is best eaten on the same day it's made.
For a posh pie, pipe the meringue with a fluted nozzle.
Freeze the spare pastry for another time.

VICTORIA SANDWICH CAKE

A traditional recipe and something we typically make in our baking class from the industrial section of our local show. At home, Joan tends to double the quantity and make two cakes, baked on the same oven shelf: one cake to eat and one for the freezer.

Preparation time: 10 minutes | Cooking time: 40 minutes | Makes 1 x 20cm cake

INGREDIENTS

180g soft margarine or butter

180g caster sugar

3 medium free-range eggs, at room temperature

180g self-raising flour

3 tablespoons raspberry jam

Whipped cream (optional)

Fresh raspberries (optional)

METHOD

Preheat the oven to 165°c. Grease and line a deep 20cm loose-bottomed cake tin with baking paper. Cream the margarine with the sugar until light and creamy in texture. Scrape down the sides of the bowl and mix until it does not feel granular.

Break the eggs into a jug and beat gently with a fork, then add in small amounts to the creamed mixture. Briskly incorporate each amount of egg with the whisk before adding the next.

Using a metal spoon, fold in the sieved flour until well combined. Scrape the mixture into the prepared tin then carefully push the mixture to the outer edges of the tin. The cake will level out during the baking process.

Bake in the oven for 40 minutes. If the sponge is browning before it is fully cooked, place a baking sheet on the shelf above the cake to shield it from the direct heat. When the cake is well risen and golden in colour, remove from the oven and leave to cool slightly in the tin, then turn out carefully and cool completely on a wire rack.

Split the cake in half and fill with the raspberry jam. Finally, sprinkle the top with some caster sugar. For an extra special teatime birthday cake, add a layer of freshly whipped cream and some fresh raspberries on top of the jam. Dust with icing sugar and add candles.

HINTS & TIPS

If you have an electric handheld whisk or mixer, this is ideal for making a lovely light sponge cake without all the hard work!

A TASTE OF CUMBRIA

Our home county produces many wonderful foods, and we wanted to showcase some of these specialities in recipes dedicated to local tastes and flavours. Solway shrimps, Cumberland sausage, mutton and lamb, game, damsons and much more from Cumbrian producers are all things we love to use in our cooking and baking. Penrith pepper is a great example of an old Westmorland recipe which traditionally would have been used in cakes as well as stews; the spices that came into Cumbria via the ports on the west coast often work well with sweet and savoury dishes, as demonstrated by our Cumberland Tarte Tatin and Penrith Peppered Lamb. Hill sheep farming has moulded our county, with native breeds grazing the high fells and shepherds using an old system of counting sheep in Cumbrian dialect. Yan means one, Tan - two, Tethera - three, then Methera, Pimp, Sethera, Lethera, Hovera, Dovera, and Dick is ten.

We've included Marmalade Ice Cream in this chapter because of its connection to Dalemain House, a stately home near Ullswater. The first marmalade festival was held there in 2005 and we were asked to be involved… despite never having made marmalade before! We enlisted Margaret's mother-in-law Laura (Gillian's mum) who was an expert on this particular preserve as well as something of a queen bee in the WI. We now make it every year following all her hints and tips, because there's no comparison between homemade and shop-bought. We're still involved with the annual festival at Dalemain too, which has become internationally recognised as the World's Original Marmalade Festival with thousands of jars entered every year and lots of money raised for a local charity.

Dalemain was where we first met Ivan Day, a local food historian who is now a regular guest tutor at Food & Co and showcases Cumbria's culinary heritage which, just like our own, is tied to the farming lifestyle. From the beginning of October to the end of January is pheasant season, and shooting is a popular Cumbrian pastime in our treasured countryside. Cooking hearty and wholesome dishes to enjoy in front of a warming fire in the bothey is something we enjoy doing each year and gives us the opportunity to cook local game, the pheasant terrine being a favourite amongst guests.

We like to celebrate these enduring connections and recipes that are passed down through the generations, making the food of our home county something really quite special.

"Yan, Tan, Tethera"

POTTED SOLWAY SHRIMPS
WITH MELBA TOASTS

These tiny shrimps bursting with flavour are caught off the north Cumbrian coast at Silloth, then boiled and hand-peeled. Local produce at its best! When cooked with butter and traditional spices, they make a simple yet classic starter that tastes truly wonderful.

Preparation time: 10 minutes | Cooking time: 10 minutes | Serves 6

INGREDIENTS

120g salted butter

½ teaspoon ground mace

¼ teaspoon ground nutmeg

¼ teaspoon cayenne pepper

Ground black pepper, to taste

250g peeled brown shrimps, defrosted

6 slices of white bread

METHOD

Gently heat the butter in a saucepan until melted. Remove from the heat and add all of the spices; don't be over generous with these though, as you can always add more later.

Return the pan to the heat and stir continuously until the butter begins to foam, then remove from the heat again and add the brown shrimps to the spiced butter.

Cover a dinner plate or similar with cling film and then spread the buttered shrimps evenly over the plate in a thin layer. Chill in the fridge until required.

For the melba toast

Toast the bread on both sides, then cut off the crusts while still warm. Lay the slices flat on a chopping board. Place your hand on top and use a serrated knife to slide through the toast horizontally, splitting the slices in two. Cut each thin slice into two triangles and toast the untoasted sides under a preheated grill until golden. Don't worry if the edges curl up, but keep your eye on them as they burn very easily. These melba toasts can be made well in advance and kept in a tin.

To serve, take the potted shrimps out of the fridge and lift the cling film to help you to break them up more easily. Divide between plates with some dressed leaves, a lemon wedge and the melba toasts.

HINTS & TIPS

For an informal starter, the potted shrimps could be served on a sharing platter along with some smoked salmon, avocado, cucumber and fresh dill to be passed around the table. It would easily serve 8 to 10 people.

PHEASANT TERRINE
WITH CUMBERLAND SAUCE

If you occasionally find a brace of pheasants left on the front doorstep, this is the recipe for you. Simply skin one of the pheasants and take off the thigh and breast meat to get roughly the quantity required. We love serving this delicious pâté after a wine tasting with our friends.

Preparation time: 30 minutes | Cooking time: 1 hour 20 minutes | Serves 12

INGREDIENTS

For the pheasant terrine

12 slices of pancetta-style streaky bacon

120g rindless, boneless belly pork, diced

2 cloves of garlic

360g pheasant meat (mixed breast and thigh)

1 teaspoon salt

Ground black pepper, to taste

1 egg

75ml Port

100ml double cream

30g butter

1 medium onion, finely diced

30g shelled pistachio nuts

15 juniper berries, crushed

1 Granny Smith apple, peeled and diced small

2 bay leaves

For the Cumberland sauce

1 orange

1 lemon

240g redcurrant jelly

1 teaspoon Dijon mustard

6 tablespoons Port

Pinch of ground ginger

Pinch of salt

Ground black pepper, to taste

METHOD

This recipe uses a 1kg loaf tin or terrine tin measuring approximately 23 by 13cm and 7cm deep. Cut a piece of baking paper large enough to cover the base and two sides with an overhang. Lay the paper flat on the worktop and cover the centre section with 10 slices of the pancetta laid side by side. Preheat the oven to 150°c.

Use a food processor to blend the belly pork with the garlic until smooth and creamy. Dice the pheasant meat evenly, add to the processor and blend until smooth. Add the salt, pepper, egg and Port then pulse to mix well. With the machine running, slowly pour in the cream. Transfer this mixture into a large bowl.

Melt the butter in a pan and fry the onion until golden and soft, then add the pistachios and juniper berries. Sauté for a couple of minutes, then leave the mixture to cool slightly before adding it to the terrine mixture along with the diced apple. Mix well until combined.

Drop the bacon-covered baking paper into the tin and then pack the pheasant mixture in. Cover with the last two slices of bacon, press the bay leaves on top and fold the overhanging baking paper over the terrine. Cover the tin with foil and place in a bain-marie.

Cook the terrine in the preheated oven for 1 hour 20 minutes, or until firm to the touch. Remove from the oven and allow to cool, leaving all of the cooking juices in the tin as most will be reabsorbed and keep the terrine moist. Weigh the terrine down with something heavy and chill overnight. Turn out of the tin and wrap in clean cling film to store.

For the Cumberland sauce

Peel the orange and lemon thinly using a potato peeler, then cut the rind into matchsticks. Cook for 5 minutes in boiling water, drain and rinse under cold running water, then drain again. Juice the orange and the lemon.

Heat the redcurrant jelly and mustard together in a pan, then add the cooked citrus rinds, juice, Port, ginger, salt and pepper. Bring to a gentle simmer and cook for just 5 minutes. When cool, pour the sauce into a lidded jar. It will keep in the fridge for several weeks.

To serve, slice the chilled terrine and garnish with a little salad, some cornichons, crusty bread and your Cumberland sauce.

BAKED RED CABBAGE WITH CHESTNUTS & VENISON SAUSAGES

Roaring log fires and a winter landscape sets the scene for this tasty, wholesome dish. Local venison sausages are wonderful but could easily be substituted with our favourite Cumberland sausage from your local butcher.

Preparation time: 20 minutes | Cooking time: 1 hour 25 minutes | Serves 6

INGREDIENTS

1 tablespoon vegetable oil

240g smoked gammon steak, diced

2 medium onions, peeled and thinly sliced

1 medium red cabbage (approx. 800g)

Small bunch of fresh thyme

400g cooking apples

50g soft brown sugar

½ teaspoon allspice

½ teaspoon ground cloves

250ml cider

2 tablespoons balsamic vinegar

Salt and ground black pepper, to taste

200g vacuum-packed chestnuts (optional)

A few sage leaves, finely sliced

12 venison sausages

METHOD

Heat the oil in a large casserole dish and fry the gammon with the onions until the meat is beginning to brown. Meanwhile, core and finely slice the cabbage. Add it to the casserole with the thyme, stirring to coat with the pan juices, then cover with a well-fitting lid and cook until the cabbage is beginning to soften. Peel, core and dice the apples.

Add the apples, sugar and spices to the casserole and cook for a further minute or two. Finally, add the cider, balsamic vinegar and seasoning. Cover again and leave to cook slowly for 35 minutes on the stove. After this time, remove the lid, increase the heat slightly and simmer for a further 5 minutes to reduce the amount of liquid. Stir in the chestnuts and sage, then transfer the mixture into a large buttered oven to table dish.

Preheat the oven to 180°c. Arrange the venison sausages neatly on the top of the cabbage mixture. Cover and bake in the preheated oven for 30 minutes. After 20 minutes, remove the lid to brown the sausages for the last 10 minutes of cooking time. Serve the dish directly from the oven with the Parsnip & Apple Mash on page 52 and a good cauliflower cheese.

HINTS & TIPS

To get ahead the cooked cabbage can be made and then cooled until required. Also, the cabbage can be frozen successfully, and when defrosted all you need to do is add the sausages and perhaps bake the dish a little longer.

STUFFED CUMBERLAND CHICKEN WITH CREAM SAUCE

We have stuffed hundreds of chicken breasts with Cumberland filling during our outside catering events; it's always a favourite for wedding celebrations and the like. The dish is also really versatile: serve it hot for dinner with friends, or chilled and sliced for a family gathering.

Preparation time: 25 minutes | Cooking time: 30-45 minutes | Serves 6

INGREDIENTS

Knob of butter

1 tablespoon vegetable oil

½ onion, finely chopped

1 stick of celery, diced

Sprig of fresh thyme

240g Cumberland sausage meat

30g fresh breadcrumbs

1 egg yolk

Salt and ground black pepper, to taste

12 dried apricots

6 chicken breasts, boneless and skinless

12 slices of thin smoked streaky bacon

1 glass of white wine

For the cream sauce

300ml dry white wine

300ml chicken stock

300ml double cream

METHOD

Heat the butter and oil in a frying pan. Stir in the onion, celery and thyme until coated and cook until they are a light golden colour. Set aside to cool while you combine the sausage meat, breadcrumbs, egg yolk and seasoning in a large bowl. Add the onion and celery mixture, including any buttery juices, but discard the woody stalks from the thyme. Use scissors to snip the apricots into small pieces and mix them into the stuffing.

Cut almost through the chicken breasts lengthways, open them out like a book and flatten to an even thickness if necessary. This is often referred to as a butterfly. Lay out all six breasts and divide the stuffing between them, spreading it evenly over the chicken. Roll up like a Swiss roll from the bottom. Wrap two pieces of streaky bacon around each breast and place in an ovenproof dish or tray. Cover and chill until needed, but remember to bring the chicken to room temperature before cooking and preheat the oven to 180°c.

Pour the glass of white wine over the stuffed and wrapped chicken, cover loosely with foil and cook in the preheated oven for 30 to 45 minutes, or until the juices from the chicken breasts run clear. Remove the foil 5 minutes before the end of the cooking time to brown them slightly. Reserve and strain the pan juices to add to the sauce, or cool and freeze for a future recipe.

Slice and serve the stuffed Cumberland chicken with the creamy white wine sauce, or if serving cold slice thinly and serve with the Cumberland sauce on page 44.

For the cream sauce

While the chicken is cooking, put the ingredients into a saucepan and bring to a simmer. Reduce the liquid by half, taking care not to boil it over. The sauce will thicken slightly, but can be thickened further with a beurre manié if desired. Leave the sauce on the light side, seasoning to taste.

To make a beurre manié, blend 15g of soft butter with a level dessertspoon of plain flour on a flat surface using a flexible palette knife. This paste can be whisked into any simmering sauce little by little until the desired thickness is reached. As the butter melts, the starch in the flour helps to thicken the liquid and the butter adds a richness and shine to the sauce.

PENRITH PEPPERED LAMB

Cumbria is renowned for quality lamb, especially the native Lakeland breeds of Herdwick and Kendal Rough Fell. The addition of an old recipe for a peppery spice blend creates a wonderfully fragrant dish.

Preparation time: 20 minutes | Cooking time: 1 hour 10 minutes | Serves 6

INGREDIENTS

For the Penrith pepper

1 tablespoon ground mace

1 tablespoon ground nutmeg

1 tablespoon ground white pepper

½ tablespoon cayenne pepper

For the casserole

Knob of butter

1 tablespoon vegetable oil

1kg lean lamb, diced

2 medium onions

2 sticks of celery

1 dessertspoon tomato purée

1 tablespoon honey

1 teaspoon salt

2 level teaspoons Penrith pepper

1 rounded tablespoon plain flour

600ml dry cider

2 bay leaves

2 sprigs of rosemary

2 dessert apples, peeled and diced
(Cox's are a great choice)

METHOD

Preheat the oven to 180°c while you make the Penrith pepper. Put all the ingredients into a lidded jar, shake and use as required. Be sure to label and date the spice blend for reference.

Heat the butter and oil in a large casserole dish. Add the diced lamb, stirring to coat and seal the meat on all sides. Peel the onions and clean the celery stalks, dice both evenly and then add them all to the browned lamb. Stir again to coat them in the meat juices and let the vegetables begin to soften.

Add the tomato purée, honey, salt and Penrith pepper to the casserole. Stir to combine and cook briefly, then sprinkle in the flour. Stir again and cook for 1 minute, allowing the flour to absorb the juices so the starch can begin to cook and in turn thicken the sauce.

Add the cider, bay leaves and rosemary. Heat until the casserole begins to simmer gently, then cover with a lid before transferring to the preheated oven. Cook for about 50 minutes, then stir in the diced apple and cook for a further 20 minutes.

Serve the lamb casserole with the Parsnip & Apple Mash and Turnip Gratin on page 52 and some green vegetables.

HINTS & TIPS

If you are cooking this to eat in the future, add the diced apple when reheating.
If you like more spice, add some extra Penrith pepper at the end of the cooking time.
Make it posh by adding poached apple rings or cooked puff pastry shapes.

TURNIP GRATIN

Just to confuse everyone, the orange swede we all know and love is referred to as a turnip in the farming communities up north. This is an unusual dish which complements lamb very well.

Preparation time: 15 minutes | Cooking time: 55 minutes | Serves 6

INGREDIENTS

600g orange swede, peeled

½ clove of garlic

Knob of butter

300ml double cream

Grated nutmeg

Salt and ground black pepper

A little parmesan cheese, grated

METHOD

Ideally, cook this in the oven at the same time as the Penrith Peppered Lamb on page 50, or preheat the oven to 180°c. Carefully cut the swede (turnip) into thin slices about 0.5cm thick, boil them in salted water for 10 minutes and drain thoroughly.

Rub the inside of a 1 litre oven to table dish with the cut edge of the garlic clove and then generously butter the dish. In a large bowl, combine the cream with the nutmeg, salt and pepper to taste. Put the turnip slices into the bowl of cream and mix well before filling the prepared oven dish. Cover with foil and cook in the preheated oven for 45 minutes.

Remove the gratin from the oven after 40 minutes, take off the foil and sprinkle some grated parmesan over the top, then bake on the top shelf for the remaining cooking time, or brown under a preheated grill.

PARSNIP & APPLE MASH

A perfect accompaniment for your favourite game recipes, or you could even serve this luxurious, slightly sweet mash with 'bangers' during the cold winter months.

Preparation time: 10 minutes | Cooking time: 30 minutes | Serves 6

INGREDIENTS

700g potatoes, peeled

350g parsnips, peeled

1 medium Cox's apple

30g butter

1 tablespoon extra virgin olive oil

2 tablespoons double cream or milk

Salt and ground white pepper, to taste

METHOD

Cut the potatoes and parsnips evenly, making the parsnips smaller. Boil them together in a large pan of salted water. Meanwhile, peel, core and dice the apple then add it to the boiling vegetables 5 minutes before they are tender. Once everything is cooked, drain well.

Return the empty pan to a gentle heat and add the butter, olive oil and cream. Once they have melted, put the drained vegetables back into the pan and mash until smooth and silky. Season to taste with salt and white pepper and transfer into a warmed serving dish.

DAMSON ICE CREAM
& MARMALADE ICE CREAM

Damsons are small local plums, vibrant and rich in flavour with an unmistakable colour. It's well worth cultivating a friendship with someone who has a damson tree in order to get your hands on a few pounds for the freezer! Our marmalade ice cream is an excellent store cupboard alternative.

Preparation time: 15 minutes, plus freezing overnight | Cooking time: 10 minutes | Serves 8

INGREDIENTS

To make damson ice cream

600g damsons

150ml water

125g sugar

300ml double cream

120g condensed milk

60g meringue, broken into chunky pieces

To make marmalade ice cream

300ml double cream

120g condensed milk

120g marmalade

2 tablespoons orange liqueur or orange juice

60g meringue, broken into chunky pieces

METHOD

For either ice cream, line a 26 by 10 by 6cm lidded plastic container or a 1kg loaf tin with cling film and leave some overhanging the sides to fold over the top.

To make damson ice cream

Put the damsons, water and sugar into a pan and simmer until soft. Use a colander over a large bowl to strain the juice from the cooked fruit. With the back of a tablespoon, push all the fruit pulp through the colander to make a thick purée and discard the stones. You should have about 600ml in total, so divide the purée into two 300ml portions, one for the ice cream and the other for a coulis, or to freeze for the next time you want to make this recipe.

In a large bowl using an electric handheld mixer, whisk the cream until it begins to thicken. Add the condensed milk and whisk briefly to combine. Gently fold in the meringue pieces with 150ml of the damson purée, then swirl the remaining 150ml of purée through the ice cream to create a ripple effect. Spoon the mixture into the prepared container, then cover with the overhanging cling film and the lid. Place in the freezer to set overnight.

Transfer the ice cream to the fridge for up to 20 minutes before serving, then turn out onto a plate, remove all the cling film and slice with a sharp knife dipped in hot water.

To make marmalade ice cream

In a large bowl using an electric handheld mixer, whisk the double cream until it begins to thicken. Add the condensed milk and whisk briefly to combine. Mix the marmalade with the orange liqueur or juice in a small bowl and use scissors to snip up any orange shreds which are too chunky. Add this mixture to the cream and whisk again so that all the ingredients are well combined and the cream has reached a medium peak stage.

Gently fold in the meringue pieces and then spoon the mixture into the prepared container. Cover the mixture with the overhanging cling film and the lid. Place in the freezer to set overnight. Serve the ice cream straight from the freezer; turn the block out onto a plate, remove all the cling film and slice with a sharp knife. For a simple dessert, serve with fresh oranges.

CUMBERLAND TARTE TATIN

This is our take on the famous Cumberland Rum Nicky recipe. We have combined the famous French classic with our traditional Cumberland classic: a marriage made in heaven! Give it a try, it is fabulous. You'll find our recipe for rum butter in the Morning Coffee, Teatime Treats chapter.

Preparation time: 15 minutes | Cooking time: 50 minutes | Serves 8

INGREDIENTS

120g rum butter (see page 22)

16 soft pitted dates

1 large piece of stem ginger in syrup, finely chopped

6 crisp dessert apples, peeled and quartered

2 tablespoons syrup from the stem ginger

2 tablespoons dark rum

320g ready-rolled puff pastry, defrosted if necessary

Grated nutmeg

METHOD

Preheat the oven to 180°c. Line a frying pan or solid-bottomed tin between 21 and 24cm in diameter with a piece of baking paper, cut to size.

Spread the rum butter over the bottom of the prepared tin and arrange the dates around the outer edge. Sprinkle the stem ginger over the rum butter in the centre of the tin.

Pack the peeled apple quarters tightly into the tin on top of the dates and ginger, curved side downwards. If you have too many pieces of apple, slice some over the top to even out the depth of fruit. Drizzle over the ginger syrup and rum.

Cook the filling in the preheated oven for 20 minutes. While the fruit is cooking, cut the puff pastry into a circle just larger than the tin and prick it all over with a fork. Lay the pastry over the hot filling, tucking in the edges as best you can. Return the tart to the oven for a further 30 minutes. After cooking, the pastry should be golden and crisp. Remove from the oven and allow to rest for 10 minutes before turning out.

Carefully invert the tart onto a large serving plate, then discard the baking paper before finishing with a little grated nutmeg. Serve slightly warm with some extra rum butter and whipped cream.

HINTS & TIPS

It is worthwhile looking out for 'all butter' puff pastry which is especially delicious in this recipe.

FOOD & CO'S
GRASMERE GINGERBREAD

It's worth visiting the Lake District just to sample Sarah Nelson's famous Grasmere Gingerbread! Old Mrs Beetham from the village always made and distributed this sweet treat to the children who took part in the Ambleside Rushbearing Ceremony. Fill your kitchen with the gorgeous aromas and have a go at making your own.

Preparation time: 15 minutes | Cooking time: 15 minutes | Makes 30 fingers

INGREDIENTS

250g shop-bought shortbread biscuits

75g Demerara sugar

30g crystallised ginger, grated

1½ level teaspoons ground ginger

30g self-raising flour

½ teaspoon baking powder

45g butter

45g golden syrup

2 teaspoons treacle

METHOD

Preheat the oven to 170°c and line an 18 by 28cm Swiss roll tin with baking paper. Roughly break the shortbread biscuits into smaller pieces and put into a processor with the Demerara sugar, crystallised ginger and ground ginger, then blend until broken into crumbs. Reserve 45g of this mixture and put the remaining crumbs into a large bowl. Add the flour and baking powder, then mix well.

Gently melt the butter, syrup and treacle in a saucepan, then pour this over the crumb mixture and stir thoroughly. Press the mixture firmly into the lined tin using a fork and then spread the reserved crumbs over the top. Use your hands to press these into the surface. Bake the gingerbread on the middle shelf of the preheated oven for about 12 to 15 minutes.

Remove from the oven and cut into fingers while still warm, then allow to cool in the tin. Once cold, cut through the original marks again and store in an airtight container.

HINTS & TIPS

This is perfect for cutting into small pieces for an after dinner treat.
Alternatively, leave in slabs, wrap in baking paper and tie with twine to make an edible gift.

A BIT OF A DO

This chapter contains our advice, or what we find works well, on putting together a successful spread for family gatherings at home. Whether the party is large or small, any combination of these recipes works well and can be prepared in advance. They can all be complemented by nice cold cuts and served alongside the salads from elsewhere in this book to give you all the elements for an informal feast.

The savoury recipes here are ideal for a 'fork buffet' with no knives required, though we do suggest having a stack of plates and plenty of napkins at the ready. This makes your table look welcoming as well as being a practical way to have people serve themselves. Individual desserts are a great idea for buffet parties; Crème Brûlée is a good example of this as it's served in its own little pot.

We've been privileged to be part of many a do within our clients' homes. Being trusted to make an event run smoothly with a memorable meal is a great responsibility, and we often felt like part of the family even though we were working on those occasions. We've hosted a fair few gatherings ourselves, of course, including two christenings for Margaret's grandchildren at her home, Matthew Rudding. Inviting people over, or going to someone's home and spending time together amongst friends is one of the things in life that Joan adores. Good people and good times deserve good food, so that's what this chapter is all about.

"Good friends, good times and good food"

PARSNIP BREAD & BUTTER BAKE

A most unusual cook now, eat later dish. Margaret always takes this to the Ridley Boxing Day lunch, a gathering of her mum-in-law's family which has been going for nearly 50 years, spanning four generations, with the host's home overflowing with 70 or more family members!

Preparation time: 30 minutes | Cooking time: 45 minutes | Serves 6

INGREDIENTS

Knob of butter

1 tablespoon vegetable oil

180g dry cured bacon, diced

1 medium onion, finely chopped

2 medium parsnips, peeled and finely sliced

Salt and ground black pepper, to taste

A grating of nutmeg

6 slices of light-textured white bread

60g soft butter

30g raisins

2 whole eggs

300ml milk

300ml double cream

75g cheddar cheese, grated

METHOD

Use the knob of butter to grease a wide, shallow 28cm casserole dish and heat the rest with the oil in a frying pan. Fry the bacon until golden brown, then use a slotted spoon to transfer it to the buttered casserole dish, leaving any oils behind. In the same pan, gently fry the onion and parsnip until cooked. Season with salt, pepper and a generous grating of nutmeg. Turn out onto a plate and allow to cool.

Butter the slices of bread on one side with the soft butter, divide the parsnip mixture between three slices and top with the remaining slices to make sandwiches, keeping the buttered side uppermost.

Carefully cut the crusts off the bread and then cut the sandwiches into triangles. Arrange them neatly in the casserole dish on top of the bacon. Gather up any parsnip or onions which have spilled from the sandwiches into the dish and scatter the raisins in and around the sandwiches.

Whisk the eggs, milk and cream together, season well with salt and pepper, then pour the mixture over the sandwiches in the dish. Top with the cheddar cheese and leave to stand for at least 1 hour before cooking.

Preheat the oven to 175°c and bake the rested pudding for about 40 to 50 minutes. It will have puffed up and look set, and the top will be golden in colour and crispy. Leave to rest for a minute or two before serving.

HINTS & TIPS

A great lunch dish served with a crisp salad.
Omit the bacon for a meatless feast.

CHICKEN ELIZABETH

This is our take on Coronation Chicken, the classic cold buffet speciality of the seventies. A delicious recipe which has now become a favourite sandwich filler, but in our opinion is best served on a platter and is still a dish fit for a queen.

Preparation time: 20 minutes | Cooking time: 25 minutes | Serves 8

INGREDIENTS

1 tablespoon vegetable oil

1 large onion, peeled and sliced

1 bay leaf

1 dessertspoon medium curry powder

75ml white wine

50ml water

1 teaspoon tomato purée

½ lemon, juiced

Salt and ground black pepper, to taste

1 tablespoon apricot jam

125ml double cream

125ml mayonnaise

6 cooked chicken breasts, diced into bite-size pieces

500g cold cooked long grain rice

2 ripe avocados (optional)

Fresh coriander, to garnish

METHOD

Heat the oil in a saucepan and fry the onion with the bay leaf until lightly coloured. Stir in the curry powder and cook for a moment. Add the wine and water which should nicely cover the onions, then add the tomato purée, lemon juice and seasoning to taste. Cover and simmer gently until the onion is soft and tender.

Take the pan off the heat and remove the bay leaf, then add the apricot jam and use a stick blender to purée the sauce until it has a smooth texture. Leave to cool and chill until required.

Whip the cream in a large bowl until fairly stiff, then add the mayonnaise and combine using a balloon whisk. Stir the chilled curry sauce into the cream and mayo and mix well.

Add the diced chicken to the creamy curry sauce and mix gently to coat all the pieces. Arrange on a large platter along with the cooked rice, chopped avocado and chopped coriander.

HINTS & TIPS
The curry sauce freezes well before the addition of cream or mayonnaise.
If you are serving this as part of a buffet party, the recipe will feed more mouths.
Red apples, sultanas and chives make great alternative garnishes to avocado and coriander.

QUICHE LORRAINE

You're bound to find quiche on the menu at any do. Everyone loves quiche with its many different fillings, which is why we always have a vegetarian option on the buffet table at our Food & Company events, made by Joan who is queen of the quiche!

Preparation time: 30 minutes | Cooking time: 1 hour 15 minutes | Serves 10 as a main, 16 as part of a buffet

INGREDIENTS

For the pastry

240g plain flour

Pinch of salt

60g block margarine

60g lard

60ml cold water

For the filling

1 tablespoon vegetable oil

2 medium onions, peeled and finely diced

360g dry cured bacon, fat removed and diced

4 large free-range eggs

250ml whole milk

250ml double cream

1 teaspoon salt

White pepper, to taste

180-240g mature coloured cheddar cheese

2 tomatoes, skinned and thinly sliced

METHOD

For the pastry

Preheat the oven to 180°c. Sift the flour and salt into a large bowl, then cut both fats into small even pieces and rub them into the flour using your fingertips until the mixture resembles breadcrumbs. Bind it together with the cold water. If time allows, let the pastry rest before using to help prevent shrinkage.

Roll out the pastry thinly and use it to line a 26cm loose-bottomed flan tin with 2cm deep sides. Let the pastry hang over the edges before pushing gently into the corner creases of the tin. Trim off the excess pastry, then cover the flan case with tin foil and fill it with baking beans. Pop the tin into the preheated oven and blind bake the pastry for about 15 minutes, followed by a further 5 minutes without the foil and baking beans.

For the filling

While the pastry case is baking, prepare the filling. Heat the oil, then fry the onions and bacon until well cooked. Drain to remove any surplus liquid and allow to cool slightly. In a separate bowl, whisk the eggs, milk, cream, salt and white pepper together.

Carefully put the bacon and onion mixture into the baked pastry case, scatter over the cheese, then pour in the egg mixture until the quiche is as full as possible without overflowing. Arrange the tomato slices around the outside edge before carefully transferring the quiche to the oven, at the same temperature you baked the pastry.

Cook the quiche for 10 minutes, then pour any leftover egg mixture into the centre and continue to cook for about 35 minutes. The quiche will be set, slightly risen and golden in colour. Serve warm or cold.

HINTS & TIPS

Use the pastry trimmings to patch up any visible holes in the case before blind baking.
The savoury custard filling has endless variations; experiment with your favourite ingredients.
If you have any concerns about the filling overflowing, put the quiche on a heavy baking tray with an edge before baking. An electric carving knife is a great way to cut the quiche.

BAKED CHICKEN GRUYÈRE

We first cooked this dish for a twenty-first birthday party and it was a roaring success, so now we use the recipe for all sorts of dos. This is a great 'cook now, eat later' supper, perfect for when you're out and about, then in need of a tasty no-fuss meal on your return.

Preparation time: 35 minutes | Cooking time: 50 minutes | Serves 6

INGREDIENTS

6 cooked chicken breasts, diced into bite-size pieces

1 packet of watercress, roughly chopped

1kg potatoes, peeled and sliced

1 clove of garlic

60g butter

70g plain flour

250ml chicken stock

250ml milk

250ml double cream

180g Gruyère cheese, grated

Salt and ground black pepper, to taste

Knob of butter, melted

METHOD

While you prepare the chicken and watercress, cook the sliced potatoes in a large pan of salted, boiling water until just tender. Drain and leave to cool.

Peel and cut the clove of garlic in half, rub the cut side over the inside of a 28cm oven-to-table casserole dish, then chop finely for the sauce. Put the diced chicken into the casserole and scatter over the watercress, then set to one side while you make the sauce.

Melt the butter in a saucepan, add the chopped garlic and cook gently for 1 minute before adding the flour. Cook for 1 more minute while stirring continuously. Combine the chicken stock and milk, then gradually add this mixture to the pan using a balloon whisk to make a smooth sauce. Finally, add the cream and heat until the sauce reaches boiling point and thickens fully. Remove from the heat and stir in the grated cheese. Season to taste with salt and pepper.

Pour the sauce over the chicken and watercress in the dish, then gently mix through to ensure the sauce is coating all the chicken pieces. Arrange the potato slices neatly on the top and brush with a small amount of melted butter. Leave to cool until required.

Bake the dish from chilled in a preheated oven at 180°c for about 50 minutes until golden in colour. Remove from the oven and rest for 5 minutes before serving with a crisp green salad.

HINTS & TIPS

The resting period is important for this dish, as it allows the sauce to thicken.

OVEN BAKED SALMON
WITH ONION MARMALADE

A whole side of salmon makes a stunning centrepiece for any table. This recipe embraces delicious citrus flavours and is a great way to pep up boring old salmon.

Preparation time: 25 minutes | Cooking time: 30 minutes | Serves 12 as part of a buffet or 6 as a main

INGREDIENTS

2 tablespoons pine nuts

4 tablespoons onion marmalade

2 fresh limes (or 50ml lime juice)

1.2kg side of salmon, skinned and pin boned

3 tablespoons tahini

Fresh coriander, to garnish

METHOD

Toast the pine nuts in a dry frying pan on a medium heat, moving them around until they become shiny and slightly darker in colour, then tip into a bowl and set aside to cool.

Cover a baking tray with edges in a double layer of tin foil big enough to wrap the whole side of salmon up. Lightly oil an area of foil in the centre equal to the size of the salmon. Spread the onion marmalade over the oiled area, scatter the toasted pine nuts on top, then zest and juice both limes over the marmalade.

Remove the thin belly section and shorten the tail of the salmon to enable it to fit on a baking tray. Season the salmon well on both sides, then lay it skinned side uppermost on the marmalade and lime mixture. Spread the tahini over the top of the salmon, then bring the edges of the foil together to enclose the salmon in a parcel. The fish can be prepared up to this stage 2 hours before cooking, but if left any longer the lime juice will begin to cure the fish.

Bake the salmon parcel for about 25 minutes in a preheated oven at 180°c. After 25 minutes, unwrap the salmon and check the middle section to make sure it is cooked. When the salmon is done, rest it for a few minutes out of the oven, then pour off any juices. Gently place a board or serving dish over the salmon and then flip the whole tray over, so the tahini is on the base and the marmalade on the top. Give the topping a little stir with a fork and serve with a good scattering of chopped coriander.

HINTS & TIPS

Try cooking the salmon parcel on the barbecue for 12 to 15 minutes over medium heat.
Edible flowers elevate this dish into something really special.

TWICE BAKED CHEESY POTATOES

A lovely addition to any buffet table, whether you're catering for a crowd or at the supper table with the family. This recipe uses simple ingredients and is a great way to get ahead of time.

Preparation time: 20 minutes | Cooking time: 1 hour 10 minutes | Serves 6-12

INGREDIENTS

7 baking potatoes

A little vegetable oil

Pinch of salt

30g soft butter

2 tablespoons crème fraîche

2 teaspoons Dijon mustard

1 medium egg

Ground black pepper, to taste

1 Camembert (approx. 250g)

90g mature cheddar cheese, grated

METHOD

Preheat the oven to 180°c. Rub the potatoes with a tiny amount of oil, place on a baking tray and sprinkle with salt. Bake in the preheated oven for about 1 hour or until the potatoes are soft.

Once they are cooked, remove from the oven and cut each one in half. Scoop the potato flesh into a large bowl but leave all the skins intact, as these will be refilled in a moment.

Add the butter to the hot potato and use a fork to mix lightly rather than mash, leaving some texture. In a separate small bowl, combine the crème fraîche with the mustard and egg, then gently stir this mixture into the buttery potato. Season well with black pepper and salt if needed.

Take the Camembert out of the fridge and use a potato peeler to remove the rind, then cut the cheese into cubes and fold them gently through the potato mixture. Fill the best 12 potato shells with the cheesy filling and then top with the grated cheddar.

Bake the filled potatoes in the oven for 10 minutes, browning under a preheated grill if required to melt the cheese. Alternatively, leave them to cool and chill in the fridge until needed, then reheat from cold in a preheated oven for about 25 minutes, or until piping hot.

HINTS & TIPS

These filled potatoes freeze very successfully, and can be reheated in the oven from frozen.
Cooked ham or bacon can also be added to the filling for a lovely change.
This recipe is a great way to use up cheeseboard leftovers.

ALMOND FILO PIE

This pie even sounds delicious when you cut into it; with crisp golden pastry and a moist, soft centre, what's not to like? Joan's daughter Sally has designated it her favourite dessert of all time. It's easy to make with store cupboard ingredients and great served with seasonal fruit.

Preparation time: 20 minutes | Cooking time: 40 minutes | Serves 10-12

INGREDIENTS

6 x 27cm sheets of filo pastry

Vegetable oil

180g soft butter

150g caster sugar

2 eggs

200g ground almonds

METHOD

Preheat the oven to 180°c and lightly grease a 25cm loose-bottomed flan tin. Working quickly so that the pastry doesn't dry out, lay the first sheet on the worktop and brush it lightly with vegetable oil, then lay into the prepared tin. Do the same with the next four sheets, laying them on top at different angles so that the base is covered evenly and there is a good excess of pastry hanging over the edge of the tin. When you have lined the tin with 5 sheets of pastry, reserve the sixth for the top of the pie.

Put the butter and sugar in a large bowl and beat with an electric handheld whisk to get a soft creamy texture. Beat in the eggs one at a time, then fold in the ground almonds. Spread the mixture over the base of the prepared pastry case.

Cut the last piece of pastry into quarters, brush with oil and use to cover the almond filling. Fold the overhanging pastry over the top of the pie to form a lid. Brush sparingly with oil.

Bake the pie in the preheated oven for about 40 minutes until golden brown. You might want to place a tray on the shelf below to catch any surplus oil. Serve warm with chilled thick cream.

HINTS & TIPS

Freeze the pie in the tin until solid, then turn out and wrap well before storing in the freezer.
To serve the pie from frozen, defrost and warm through in a preheated oven.

STRAWBERRIES WITH BEAUJOLAIS & BLACK PEPPER SYRUP

Summertime, and the living is easy… You'll be singing with happiness after you've tasted this syrup in the sunshine! Perfect served over seasonal strawberries or good vanilla ice cream.

Preparation time: 5 minutes | Cooking time: 20 minutes | Makes 250ml

INGREDIENTS

500ml Beaujolais wine

15-20 peppercorns, roughly crushed

7cm cinnamon stick

150g caster sugar

1 punnet of strawberries

METHOD

Put all the ingredients except the strawberries into a pan and bring to the boil. Reduce the heat slightly and simmer for 20 minutes or until the syrup has reduced by half. Cool and strain into a screw top jar with a lid. It will keep for several weeks in the fridge.

Fill a pretty serving bowl with hulled and halved strawberries, then pour over the syrup just before serving, or serve alongside in a jug or a glass bottle.

CRÈME BRÛLÉE

A smooth, rich and delicious custard using the freshest free-range eggs and vanilla is unveiled when you break through the brittle sugary topping. This is a great recipe for any cook who gets the jitters when making this classic dessert, helping you feel more confident with great results.

Preparation time: 15 minutes | Cooking time: 30-40 minutes | Serves 6-10

INGREDIENTS

4 free-range egg yolks

1 tablespoon caster sugar

2 teaspoons vanilla extract

600ml whipping cream

6 dessertspoons Demerara sugar

METHOD

Preheat the oven to 140°c. Place 6 normal ramekins or 10 mini ones into a roasting tin. Put the egg yolks into a large bowl, add the caster sugar and the vanilla extract, then mix together thoroughly using a balloon whisk.

Heat the cream in a saucepan until just under boiling point, then pour it in a steady stream onto the egg mixture while whisking continuously. Once combined, pour the custard through a sieve back into the pan and heat gently once more until just below boiling point. Immediately pour the custard into a jug to prevent the eggs cooking any further.

Fill the ramekins with the custard, then half fill the roasting tin with water from a just-boiled kettle. Cook on the middle shelf of the preheated oven for about 30 to 40 minutes. They need to be set, but still have a wobble. When done, carefully place the ramekins on a dry tea towel and then onto an ovenproof tray. Allow to cool fully, then cover and chill until required.

A couple of hours before serving, sprinkle the pots of custard generously with the Demerara sugar and place the tray under a very hot grill. Watch them carefully and remove when the sugar melts and takes on a slightly burnt appearance. When completely cold, put them back into the fridge uncovered. Serve the crème brûlée straight from the fridge.

RICH CHOCOLATE SLICE

Many years ago, a dinner party birthday celebration was held at Crossrigg Hall and this delicious chocolate dessert was served, made to a recipe handed down by their late dear mother. We've slightly adapted the recipe and created this indulgent version which has appeared at numerous marquee weddings.

Preparation time: 30 minutes | Serves 12

INGREDIENTS

420g chocolate (54% cocoa solids)

75g butter

150g digestive biscuits, finely crushed

300ml double cream

2 teaspoons coffee granules

4 tablespoons boiling water

2 tablespoons dark rum

2 tablespoons brandy

2 egg yolks

METHOD

Loosely oil a 20cm round springform tin and line the base and sides with parchment paper, using a bit of butter to make it stick if needed. Break the chocolate into small pieces and put them into a large bowl over a pan of simmering water to gently melt.

Melt the butter in a saucepan, then stir in the crushed biscuits and mix really well. Turn out into the prepared tin and spread evenly over the base, pressing the biscuit mixture down firmly using your fingertips. Place in the fridge to chill.

Whip 100ml of the double cream until it is quite firm, dot evenly over the biscuit base, then carefully spread the cream out to form an even layer. Return the tin to the fridge.

Stir the chocolate until thoroughly melted. In a jug, combine the coffee granules with the boiling water and mix until dissolved, then stir in the rum and brandy. Pour this mixture into the chocolate and mix well using a balloon whisk. Next, add the egg yolks one at a time and whisk until blended. Finally, whip the remaining cream until a soft peak stage is reached, carefully fold the cream into the chocolate mixture, then simply scrape this onto the cream layer in the tin and tap to level. Return the dessert to the fridge to chill.

Decorate the set chocolate slice with grated chocolate and edible gold spray or glitter, then serve in small slices with extra cream and fresh berries. This dessert is best brought to room temperature before serving.

HINTS & TIPS

Use a sharp knife, dipped in hot water and dried, to cut neat slices. This dessert freezes really well, and you can also freeze the leftover egg whites for meringues (just remember to label them). To make a darker, more intense version of this dessert, simply reduce the amount of double cream at the end of the recipe from 200ml to 150ml.

AL FRESCO

Despite the shortcomings of our Cumbrian weather, we love picnics and any other opportunities to eat al fresco which translates as 'in the open air' and specifically means to dine outdoors. The lockdown in the spring and summer of 2020 inspired this chapter, because we couldn't hold events indoors and the weather was unexpectedly brilliant for the most part. Once we were allowed to have people round in the garden, there were many occasions where our families joined us to enjoy pizza, paella, sangria and lemonade in the sunshine.

Ian and Richard, our husbands and great friends, are always put on barbecue duty at these gatherings which they do rather well at. We also learnt how to make our own pizza on the barbecue which is a fantastic alternative to takeaways. Joan's daughter Sarah even threw a pizza party for her husband Tom's birthday; letting your friends choose their own toppings and line up to have their dinner cooked right in front of them is a great idea and would make a memorable occasion for young ones and oldies alike!

Part of our affection for picnic recipes comes from nostalgia, although they weren't as elaborate in those days; we have very fond memories of childhood picnics in the hayfield featuring tea in a tin and Mum's elderflower champagne. To this day, Margaret's birthday is celebrated with a picnic whether there's rain, gales or even a bit of sun… without fail, Margaret and Richard have a picnic with their friends (who share a wedding anniversary on the same date in August) which has taken place on top of the fell, at the bottom of the fell amongst the gorse, under a bridge by the river or in any old shelter! It's become a much-loved tradition that often ends in stargazing.

To round off these al fresco recipes, we've chosen three light, fruity desserts and two drinks, one alcoholic and one not, to make the most of the warmer season's bounty and the delights of outdoor dining, whatever the weather.

> "If you can't see the fells it's raining, if you can see the fells it's going to rain"

SCOTCH EGGS

A hassle-free picnic food that is both filling and transportable. All you need is a sharp knife, some salt and a jar of chutney. Boris brought the humble scotch egg to fame as a "substantial meal" to have at the pub with a pint during the pandemic of 2020.

Preparation time: 25 minutes, plus 20 minutes chilling | Cooking time: 12-15 minutes | Makes 6

INGREDIENTS

6 small or medium-size eggs

500g Cumberland sausagemeat

2 teaspoons cornflour

1 teaspoon English mustard powder

1 tablespoon chopped fresh parsley

½ teaspoon salt

2 tablespoons plain flour

1 teaspoon paprika

1 teaspoon salt

1 egg, beaten with a little milk

Panko breadcrumbs

Oil, for deep frying

METHOD

Place the eggs in a single layer in a pan and add enough cold water to cover them. Prepare a bowl of iced water while you bring the eggs to the boil quickly. Once boiling, remove the pan from the heat and leave the eggs to stand for 5 minutes. Transfer the eggs from the hot water into the iced water and leave for 15 minutes. If you prefer a set yolk, hard-boil the eggs for 5 to 8 minutes instead.

Place the sausagemeat into a processor with the cornflour, mustard, chopped parsley and ½ teaspoon of salt. Blitz everything together and then divide into seven portions. Lay out six pieces of cling film and place a portion of sausagemeat on each. Place a second piece of cling film on top of the sausagemeat and flatten into circles large enough to surround an egg. Remove the top piece of cling film and discard.

Carefully peel the eggs using a teaspoon if necessary, then place an egg in the centre of each sausagemeat circle and, using the cling film to assist you, wrap the sausagemeat around the egg. Use some of the spare sausagemeat to cover any exposed egg, then bring the cling film around the egg and twist the top to ensure the sphere holds its shape. Chill for at least 20 minutes.

Preheat the oven to 180°c. Put the plain flour, paprika and teaspoon of salt onto a plate and mix well, then unwrap each scotch egg and roll in the seasoned flour. Next, roll the eggs in the beaten egg and milk mixture then coat completely in breadcrumbs. Repeat this process for a second time, gently pressing the breadcrumbs into the sausagemeat with your hands.

Using a deep fat fryer or a deep saucepan, heat the oil to 190°c. Fry the scotch eggs two at a time for about 2 minutes until golden brown. Carefully remove them from the oil with a slotted spoon and place on a wire rack over an oven tray. When all of the eggs have been fried, cook in the preheated oven for about 10 minutes. Allow to cool and then chill until required.

PICNIC LOAF

The thought of picnic baskets, blankets, chilled drinks and flasks of tea evoke many childhood memories. But our family picnics never had any sandwiches as complex as this wonderfully packed loaf. Also called a pan bagnat, this is a thing of beauty once cut open.

Preparation time: 30 minutes | Serves 6

INGREDIENTS

1 large white country-style loaf

4 tablespoons pesto

4 tablespoons vinaigrette

3 tomatoes

200g roasted peppers from a jar

100g garlicky salami

70g black olives, pitted

200g cooked ham, thinly sliced

Rocket leaves

METHOD

Slice off the top of the loaf and carefully remove the centre of the bread, leaving a hollow shell 1 to 2cm thick. Turn the removed centre into breadcrumbs using a food processor and divide these evenly between two bowls. Mix one half with the pesto and the other half with the vinaigrette.

Slice the tomatoes and place them onto absorbent paper with the peppers. Add each ingredient to the hollow loaf in layers, gently firming each layer using your hands. For a great visual effect, layer the loaf in the following order: two thirds of the pesto crumbs, the sliced salami, tomatoes and black olives, then the vinaigrette crumbs, sliced ham, rocket and roasted peppers. Finally, fill the hollow with the remaining pesto crumbs.

Replace the 'lid' of the loaf and place onto a piece of baking paper about 33cm square. Secure with some cooking bands, then place the wrapped loaf in the centre of a muslin cloth. Tie the opposite corners firmly together so that the muslin is tight and secure.

Leave the picnic loaf in the fridge overnight, using an upturned plate and bowl to lightly weigh it down. This will help compress the layers and make the loaf easy to cut. To serve, unwrap on a wooden board and cut into wedges using a serrated knife.

PESTO

Versatile and better than any shop-bought version, vividly green and a great thing to make yourself. Try using wild garlic leaves when in season instead of basil.

Preparation time: 10 minutes | Makes 300ml

INGREDIENTS

60g pine nuts

2 cloves of garlic

60g parmesan cheese

50-60g basil leaves

8 tablespoons extra virgin olive oil

¼ teaspoon salt

Black pepper, to taste

METHOD

Gently warm the pine nuts in a dry frying pan. Once they begin to look glossy, put them into a food processor. Peel the garlic, grate the parmesan, add both to the processor and blend until the ingredients are finely chopped and granular.

Add the basil, including any soft stalks, then with the processor running add the olive oil in a slow steady stream until the pesto has a slightly grainy texture and is a wonderful green colour. Season to taste and put into a lidded jar. Top with a little more oil and store in the fridge until required.

HOMITY PIE

There are many versions of this delicious pie consisting of onions, potatoes and cheese. Simple and irresistible, this pie makes a great alternative to quiche. Cut into small wedges and wrap in tin foil for an on-the-move meal or picnic.

Preparation time: 45 minutes | Cooking time: 1 hour 35 minutes | Serves 8

INGREDIENTS

For the pastry

240g plain flour

Pinch of salt

60g block margarine

60g lard

60ml cold water

For the filling

1kg baking potatoes

240g onion

2 cloves of garlic

1 teaspoon salt

60g butter

Black pepper, to taste

300g mature cheddar cheese

METHOD

Preheat the oven to 180°c. Bake the potatoes in the oven until soft, then leave to one side.

For the pastry

Sift the flour and salt into a large bowl. Cut the fats into even pieces and rub into the flour until it resembles breadcrumbs. Add the water and mix together using a round-bladed knife until a dough is formed.

On a lightly floured surface, roll out sufficient pastry into a circle large enough to line a 24cm loose-bottomed flan tin (surplus pastry can be frozen for another time). Using foil and baking beans, bake blind for about 15 minutes, then remove from the oven and take the foil and beans away. Bake for another 5 minutes until the pastry is fully cooked.

For the filling

Peel the skins off the baked potatoes and cut the flesh into chunky pieces. Peel and dice the onion and crush the garlic with the salt, then melt the butter in a saucepan and fry both until soft. Add the cooked potatoes and stir until combined, but be careful not to mash them. Season with black pepper before removing from the heat. Add 150g of the cheese to the pan and mix gently.

Cover the bottom of the pastry case with 75g of the remaining cheese. Top with the potato mixture and spread out evenly, then scatter the remaining cheese over the top.

Return to the preheated oven on a baking tray to collect any excess oil and bake for about 35 minutes until the pie is cooked through and the cheese topping is golden. This pie is lovely served warm but is equally delicious cold.

PIZZA ON THE GRILL

Restaurant quality pizza at home on the gas barbecue. Children and grownups alike will love this al fresco occasion. Be sure to have a stash of dough bases, pizza sauce and toppings ready to go in the fridge. Let the pizza party begin!

Preparation time: 25 minutes, plus 1 hour proving | Cooking time: 8 minutes | Makes 6 x 20cm pizzas

INGREDIENTS

For the pizza sauce

1 tablespoon olive oil

2 cloves of garlic, crushed

1 small onion, finely chopped

500g passata

1 small tin of tomato purée (142g)

2 teaspoons sugar

2 teaspoons dried oregano

Salt and black pepper, to taste

For the dough

360g strong plain flour

1 sachet of fast-action bread yeast (7g)

1 teaspoon white sugar

½ teaspoon salt

60ml olive oil

240ml tepid water

For the toppings

Cheddar and/or mozzarella, grated

Cooked ham and/or air-dried ham

Pepperoni and/or salami

Black olives

Mushrooms

Peppers

Fresh basil

METHOD

For the pizza sauce

Fry the garlic and onion in the olive oil for 5 minutes until golden, then add all the other ingredients to the pan. Stir well and cover loosely with some tin foil, as the sauce may spit a little, then gently simmer for 5 minutes. Check the seasoning, cool and then chill until required.

For the dough

Put all of the dry ingredients into a large bowl, then add the olive oil and water and mix until a soft dough is formed. Knead for 10 minutes on a work surface until the dough is smooth, or 5 minutes if using a stand mixer. Return the dough to the bowl, cover and leave for at least 1 hour to rise.

Once well risen, knock the dough back and then divide into six equal pieces. Using a little flour and a rolling pin, shape and flatten each piece to achieve a thin base of about 20cm in diameter. It's best to roll each base in turn and repeat the process until you achieve the correct shape and size.

Preheat a gas barbecue to a medium heat. Brush one side of the uncooked pizza base with a little olive oil and grill in batches for 3 to 5 minutes each, oiled side down, directly on the barbecue grid with the lid down. If any air pockets form as they cook, prick them with a fork. At this point the bases can be cooled, stacked and covered, then stored in the fridge until required.

Transfer the cooked bases to a tray with the grilled side of the pizza facing upwards. Spread the pizza sauce over the surface, leaving a 1cm edge to form the crust, then add the cheese. Use your favourite toppings to complete your pizza.

Return the pizzas to the barbecue on a medium to hot heat. Cook with the lid closed for about 5 minutes until the pizzas are crisp on the bottom and piping hot. Enjoy straight from the grill, with your pizza wheel at the ready.

HINTS & TIPS

Any spare pizza sauce and cooked bases can be frozen.
If it's not barbecue weather, the bases can be cooked on a solid griddle on the stove top and the pizzas can be finished off in a hot oven.

TUSCAN STEAK

This is a meat lover's delight and an easy and different way to serve succulent and juicy steaks. Cumbria is renowned for beef farming and we are lucky to have an abundance of excellent butchers who buy from local farms. It's great served with the Greek potato salad below.

Preparation time: 5 minutes | Cooking time: 10-15 minutes | Serves 2

INGREDIENTS

1 sirloin steak, thick cut (approx. 3cm) and weighing approx. 400g

Oil, to rub the steak

Salt and black pepper

1 lemon, juiced

2 tablespoons chopped fresh parsley

METHOD

Preheat the barbecue, making sure the rack is clean. Rub the steak with a little oil on each side and season generously with salt and pepper.

Put the steak on the hot barbecue and close the lid. Set a timer for exactly 4 minutes before turning over and cooking for another 4 minutes on the other side. Yes, it's that easy. Try to resist lifting the lid before the time is up. No peeking or turning the meat over several times. Be patient and you will be rewarded. For a well-done steak, extend the cooking time.

When the steak has finished cooking, move it onto a piece of foil and scatter with chopped parsley and the lemon juice. Make a parcel using the foil to enclose the steak and allow it to rest for another 3 minutes.

Open the parcel, reserving any meat juices which have collected. Discard the foil and put the steak onto a board. Carve the sirloin diagonally into thin slices and arrange on a warm serving plate. Spoon over the reserved juices and serve immediately.

GREEK POTATO SALAD

Preparation time: 10 minutes | Serves 6

INGREDIENTS

500g cooked new potatoes

3 spring onions, sliced

100g feta cheese, crumbled

1 teaspoon capers, chopped

1 tablespoon each of chopped fresh dill and parsley

½ lemon, zested

170g Greek yoghurt

2 tablespoons olive oil

1 teaspoon wholegrain mustard

Salt and black pepper, to taste

METHOD

Cut the cooked potatoes into even, bite-size pieces and gently combine in a bowl with the sliced spring onions, crumbled feta and chopped capers.

Mix the dill and parsley in a large bowl with the lemon zest, yoghurt, olive oil and wholegrain mustard, then season with salt and pepper.

Add the potato mixture to the dressing and gently stir until everything is well coated before spooning the salad into a serving bowl.

If you like, garnish the salad with either sliced or quartered hard-boiled eggs, halved olives and more fresh parsley.

PAELLA

Taking advantage of the gorgeous weather during the first lockdown, we often rustled up this fabulous one-pot recipe for our family bubbles in the garden. Over the years, paella has featured on many occasions including wedding receptions, corporate events and cookery demonstrations at Food & Company.

Preparation time: 20 minutes | Cooking time: 30 minutes | Serves 6-8

INGREDIENTS

2 onions

4 cloves of garlic

250g chorizo

3 chicken breasts, skinless and boneless

300g button mushrooms

3 red peppers

240g frozen peas

Large pinch of saffron

500g paella rice

45g butter

3 tablespoons vegetable oil

1 teaspoon smoked paprika

Salt and black pepper, to taste

1 glass of dry white wine

1 litre good chicken stock

250g large raw peeled prawns

Fresh parsley, chopped

2 lemons, cut into wedges

METHOD

Peel and finely dice the onions, crush the garlic, dice or slice the chorizo, dice the chicken into roughly 2.5cm pieces, wipe and slice the mushrooms, deseed and dice the peppers and defrost the peas. When all the ingredients are prepared, arrange them on a large tray or platter. Soak the saffron in a small amount of hot water and leave to infuse. Rinse and drain the paella rice. It is really beneficial to have all of the ingredients prepared and ready to add to the paella in turn before you start cooking.

If you have one, put a 40 to 46cm paella pan on a medium heat. Melt the butter and oil in the paella pan, then add the onions, garlic and chorizo. Fry until golden, stirring continuously. Add the chicken with the smoked paprika and fry until the meat has sealed on all sides. Add the mushrooms and red peppers, stir through and season generously with salt and pepper.

Add the rice and stir through to coat with the buttery vegetables and chicken. Add the wine and allow the liquid to evaporate before adding the saffron and chicken stock all at once. Stir and then adjust the heat to a gentle simmer, stirring occasionally to ensure the paella doesn't stick.

After 15 minutes, when most of the stock has been absorbed, add the prawns and peas. Stir to combine and cook gently for a further 5 minutes. Taste to check the rice is almost cooked and that the seasoning is sufficient. Turn off the heat, cover the pan with a tray or tin foil and leave the paella to stand for 5 minutes. This allows the rice to steam until done.

Scatter a good amount of chopped parsley over the paella, then add lemon wedges. Guests can serve themselves straight from the pan which is perfect for a summer al fresco supper; all you need alongside is a basket of crusty bread.

HINTS & TIPS

Use long grain rice if paella rice is unavailable.

BAKED PEACHES WITH AMARETTO & MARSALA

A truly seasonal recipe for when peaches are abundant. Use slightly firm fruits to retain the plump texture of the flesh. The secret ingredient is a splash of Marsala, worthy of a place in the drinks cabinet.

Preparation time: 10 minutes | Cooking time: 20 minutes | Serves 6

INGREDIENTS

24 amaretto biscuits

50g granulated sugar

30g dark chocolate chips

30g blanched almonds, chopped

3 tablespoons Marsala wine, plus extra to taste

6 ripe peaches

METHOD

Preheat the oven to 160°c. Crumble the biscuits into a bowl, then add the sugar, chocolate chips and almonds. Mix thoroughly, then add some Marsala to moisten the mixture and set aside.

Use peaches that can be easily halved and remove their stones before sitting them cut side up in an ovenproof dish. If the peaches wobble in the dish, cut a flat base so they sit stably. Top the peach halves with the biscuit mixture and pour a little more Marsala around them.

Bake uncovered in the preheated oven for about 20 minutes. If the peaches are still firm after this time, bake for an extra 5 minutes.

Serve warm with Greek yoghurt or vanilla ice cream. Fresh raspberries are also especially delicious with this dessert.

HINTS & TIPS

If peaches are not available, you can try using nectarines instead.

HONEY POACHED PINEAPPLE WITH PASSIONFRUIT CREAM

*We are very lucky to frequently receive a jar of delicious Mirehouse honey.
Cooked pineapple is unusual but it really allows the honey notes to shine through,
making for a light and refreshing treat on a summer's day.*

Preparation time: 20 minutes | Cooking time: 15 minutes | Serves 4

INGREDIENTS

1 medium-size ripe pineapple

1 lime

200ml pineapple juice

3 tablespoons runny honey

For the passionfruit cream

150ml natural yoghurt

150ml double cream

1 dessertspoon caster sugar

3 passionfruit

METHOD

Use a sharp knife to slice the top and base off the pineapple, then cut off the skin and remove the eyes. Cut the pineapple into quarters lengthways, remove the core from each piece and discard, then slice each piece in half lengthways again to make eight long wedges.

Put the pineapple into a wide, shallow pan in a single layer. Remove the zest from the lime using a potato peeler and add to the pan. Next, add the fruit juice and honey, cover with a lid and gently simmer for about 15 minutes. Lift out the pineapple with a slotted spoon and put into a lidded container. Return the pan to the heat and boil the juice rapidly. When it turns syrupy, pour over the pineapple, allow to cool, then chill.

For the passionfruit cream

Put the yoghurt, cream and sugar into a bowl and whip with an electric handheld whisk until it begins to thicken. Halve two passionfruit, scoop out the flesh (juice, seeds and pulp) and stir it into the yoghurt mixture. Once fully combined, place in a serving bowl and spoon over the flesh of the remaining passionfruit. Chill until required.

Serve the pineapple wedges from a pretty serving bowl with a dollop of passionfruit cream and a drizzle of syrup. The pineapple takes on a beautiful deep golden colour.

HINTS & TIPS

Apple juice can be used as an alternative to pineapple juice.

LEMON POTS

It only takes three ingredients to make this luxurious dessert, which is clean on the palate and marries well with fresh raspberries. For an on-the-go feast, use small jam jars or pots and add fresh fruit before putting on the lid. Genius!

Preparation time: 15 minutes, plus chilling overnight | Cooking time: 5 minutes | Makes 6

INGREDIENTS

2 lemons

600ml double cream

150g caster sugar

METHOD

Finely grate the zest from one lemon into a small bowl, add the juice of both lemons and put to one side.

In a large pan, heat the cream and sugar. Stir until the sugar has dissolved and then bring to a rolling boil. Boil for exactly 3 minutes without stirring. It is essential to use double cream for this recipe to be successful and also a large pan so that the cream does not boil over.

After the 3 minutes, remove from the heat and stir in the lemon zest and juice. Pour the hot lemon cream into a jug and divide it between 6 small jam jars or ramekins. Allow to cool and then chill overnight.

These lemon pots are great served with some fresh raspberries or a fruit compôte on the side and a homemade shortbread biscuit.

HINTS & TIPS

Use up leftover double cream and freeze the Lemon Pots.

Serve in shot glasses to make one of the elements for a trio of desserts.

WHITE SANGRIA

A very useful recipe for a hot summer's day. If you feel the need to make the Sangria more alcoholic, just swap the lemonade for a bottle of Spanish Cava. That will do the trick!

Preparation time: 5 minutes | Serves 10

INGREDIENTS

50ml brandy or triple sec

1 lemon, juiced

2 tablespoons sugar

3 peaches

1 bottle of dry white Spanish wine, chilled (75cl)

½ litre lemonade, chilled

Ice cubes

Mint sprigs

METHOD

Using a suitable container, combine the brandy, lemon juice, and sugar. Slice the peaches and add them to the brandy before leaving to marinate for about 1 hour. Add the dry white wine and lemonade as your guests arrive.

To serve, put ice cubes and mint sprigs in the glasses. Transfer the white sangria into a pitcher and pour. We love to use giant ice cubes as they do not water down the drinks. Just make sure they fit in the glasses!

HOMEMADE LEMONADE

A grown-up lemonade that quenches your thirst on those long, hot summer days.

Preparation time: 10 minutes | Cooking time: 10 minutes | Makes 600ml syrup

INGREDIENTS

8 unwaxed lemons

30g fresh ginger

240g granulated sugar

300ml water

Sparkling water, chilled

Ice cubes

Mint sprigs

METHOD

Using a potato peeler, remove the zest from two of the lemons and slice the ginger. Place the zest and ginger into a medium-size pan with the sugar and water, then bring to boiling point. Simmer for 10 minutes until it becomes a light syrup, then leave to cool.

Juice all 8 of the lemons, which should give you about 300ml of lemon juice. Add the juice to the syrup and then strain into a jug. Decant the lemon syrup into a bottle and chill until required.

To serve, mix the lemon syrup with chilled sparkling water at a ratio of about 1 part syrup to 3 parts sparkling water. Serve over ice cubes and decorate with fresh mint.

LADIES WHO LUNCH

This chapter is structured slightly differently than the rest, with four menus inspired by the cuisines of France, Italy, Spain and Thailand. It's a template for an interesting evening at home, combining three courses that you could make for friends or family in your own kitchen. Each of the four menus comprises a starter and main dish that could be rounded off beautifully with the desserts we have suggested on the main course recipes, which are featured elsewhere in the book. Of course, the recipes in this chapter can also be enjoyed separately for any occasion.

We have also included a wine pairing for each dish, provided by Nick Shill who runs his own local wine bar, deli and wine shop with his wife Wendy. He leads our 'ladies who lunch' themed event at Mirehouse, which offers a wine tasting session in the morning, then a sit-down lunch during which the same wines are matched with selected dishes so people can appreciate them fully. It's a summertime event and our guests love to get dressed up, often finding themselves reliving their youth and letting their hair down. We call this education by inebriation!

We love food, we love wine, and we love enjoying them together, whether with the Cumbria Wine Society or our group of friends and family lovingly known as the 'wine slurpers'. We want people to branch out in their tastes, discover wines which are new to them and have some fun. We do run other Food & Company wine and food pairing events that aren't just for ladies too!

"Education by inebriation"

COFFEE KEEPS ME GOING TILL IT IS ACCEPTABLE TO DRINK WINE

CHICKEN LIVER PARFAIT

As smooth and luxurious as they come, this recipe seems complex but is easy and well worth a try. Parfait makes a lovely hassle-free starter, as it's best made a couple of days in advance.

Preparation time: 15 minutes | Cooking time: 40 minutes | Serves 6

INGREDIENTS

60ml brandy

60ml dry white wine

Sprig of fresh thyme

240g chicken livers

1 large egg

½ teaspoon salt

White pepper, to taste

120g salted butter

1 bay leaf

METHOD

Preheat the oven to 160°c. Line a loaf tin or terrine tin measuring approximately 16 by 9cm and 6cm deep with baking paper.

Measure the brandy and wine into a small saucepan, add the thyme and bring to the boil. Simmer to reduce the liquid by half, then remove the pan from the heat and discard the thyme.

Check the livers for any discoloured areas or bile sacks, removing and discarding these. Place the livers into a food processor with a metal blade. Add the egg and reduced alcohol, season with the salt and white pepper, then blend briefly. Melt the butter in a small pan, then with the machine running add the butter to the processor in a steady stream until you have a purée.

Pour the parfait mixture into a sieve over a bowl and push it through with the back of a spoon to achieve a velvety smooth texture. Transfer the mixture into the lined tin, place the bay leaf on top and fold over any surplus baking paper to cover the surface.

Put the tin into a roasting tray and pour hot water into the tray until it comes halfway up the tin. Cover the whole tray with foil and cook in the preheated oven for about 40 minutes, or until the parfait is firm to touch.

Allow the parfait to cool slightly, then place another tin on top with some added weight in to gently press down on the parfait. Chill in the fridge overnight. Once cold, turn it out of the tin, discard the baking paper, and wrap the parfait in cling film then foil. Keep in the fridge until required.

To serve, slice the parfait using a hot sharp knife for a clean finish. Garnish the plates with a few cornichons, salad leaves and some lovely crusty French bread.

WINE NOTES

No need to spend a fortune here. I would head straight to the south of France and look at reds from the Languedoc. Our personal favourites tend to come from Minervois and the surrounding villages. They are generally unoaked and feature Syrah, Grenache Noir, Mourvèdre and Carignan. A couple of weeks touring this area is captivating. Chicken Liver Parfait needs to be paired with something that won't overpower it, so Beaujolais would work too.

COQ AU VIN

A classic French pot roast, simple but delicious. We like to use a whole chicken,
jointed into twelve pieces, but if you don't like bones just buy boneless meat
and reduce the cooking time. Our suggested dessert for this menu would be
the Crème Brûlée (see page 76).

Preparation time: 30 minutes | Cooking time: 1 hour 15 minutes | Serves 6

INGREDIENTS

2 tablespoons vegetable oil

150g bacon lardons

300g carrots

12 shallots or button onions

2 cloves of garlic, crushed

240g button mushrooms

12 pieces of chicken, skin on

300ml chicken stock

300ml burgundy wine

1 bouquet garni

Salt and black pepper, to taste

Fresh parsley, to garnish

METHOD

Preheat the oven to 160°c and heat the oil in a large casserole. Fry the
lardons until crispy, stirring often. Peel the carrots and shallots, cut the
carrots into chunky pieces and leave the shallots whole, then add both to
the casserole. Stir to coat the vegetables with the oils and fry until
beginning to colour lightly. Add the garlic and mushrooms (cleaned if
necessary) to the pot and fry for a moment before using a slotted spoon to
transfer the vegetable mixture onto a plate.

Add a little extra oil to the casserole and seal the chicken pieces on all
sides. Put them on a plate and place half of the vegetables and lardons
back into the casserole, then put the chicken pieces on top, followed by
the remaining vegetable mixture. Pour the stock and wine over the chicken,
add the bouquet garni and season well. Cover with a well-fitting lid and
cook in the preheated oven for 50 minutes, or until the chicken is cooked
through.

Carefully pour the cooking liquid from the casserole into a saucepan and
bring to the boil. Discard the bouquet garni and thicken the sauce slightly
using a beurre manié if desired. Taste to check the seasoning and return
the sauce to the casserole. Put the coq au vin back in the oven for a final
10 minutes to ensure it is piping hot.

Garnish with chopped parsley and serve alongside baby potatoes and fine
green beans.

To make a beurre manié, blend 15g of soft butter with a level dessertspoon
of plain flour on a flat surface using a flexible palette knife. This paste can
be whisked into any simmering sauce little by little until the desired
thickness is reached. As the butter melts, the starch in the flour helps to
thicken the liquid and the butter adds a richness and shine to the sauce.

WINE NOTES

For many people, France is the epicentre of food and wine production. This dish is one of those that captures the very
essence of French cookery. Red burgundy is the go-to choice but can be on the pricey side with the big names at well
over £60 or £70 a bottle… ouch! Try one of the Beaujolais villages like Fluerie, Morgon, Brouilly or Moulin au Vent
instead; still pricey but a real treat!

OVEN BAKED FRITTATA

Simple ingredients really make this classic Italian starter. It's easy to make ahead, easy to serve and even easier to eat! Perfect for ladies who lunch.

Preparation time: 20 minutes | Cooking time: 30 minutes | Serves 10 or 6 as a main course

INGREDIENTS

2 tablespoons olive oil

2 large onions, sliced

400g cooked potatoes

60g parmesan cheese

4 large eggs

1 teaspoon salt

¼ teaspoon white pepper

METHOD

Preheat the oven to 160°c. Heat the oil in a frying pan, add the sliced onions and cook until beginning to colour and soften, then remove from the heat.

Thinly slice the potatoes and grate the parmesan. Break the eggs into a large bowl and beat using a fork. Add the cooked onion, sliced potatoes and three quarters of the grated cheese to the egg, combine all the ingredients thoroughly, then add the seasoning.

Grease and line the base of a 20cm solid-bottomed flan tin or a small frying pan with olive oil and baking paper. Pour in the frittata mixture and sprinkle the remaining cheese over the top. Bake in the preheated oven for about 30 minutes or until set. Leave to cool slightly before turning out of the tin.

Serve the frittata at room temperature, cut into wedges and garnished with a tomato and basil salad. You could even add some Parma ham and perhaps some shaved parmesan cheese.

WINE NOTES

Champagne is probably the dream wine match here. Fizz always goes well with eggs, but we are going to stick our necks out and suggest Pignoletto. This could be the next rising star after Prosecco and it works so well with the fatty richness of a cooked egg dish. Pignoletto is produced near Bologna in relatively small amounts; perfect for a lunch party!

BAKED COD WITH FENNEL & CANNELLINI BEANS

A bed of vegetables is a great way to cook fillets of fresh fish. This is Italy on a plate.
All you require is a basket of ciabatta bread to mop up the fabulous juices.
Our suggested dessert for this menu would be the Baked Peaches with
Amaretto & Marsala (see page 94).

Preparation time: 40 minutes | Cooking time: 1 hour 15 minutes | Serves 6

INGREDIENTS

3 small fennel bulbs

2 x 220g tins of cannellini beans

750g fresh tomatoes

2 bay leaves

2 sprigs of rosemary

2 cloves of garlic, sliced

Pinch of saffron filaments, soaked in a little hot water

4 tablespoons vermouth or white wine

250ml vegetable stock

3 tablespoons olive oil

2 tablespoons crème fraîche

1 teaspoon cornflour

Salt and black pepper, to taste

6 x 180g portions of cod loin, skin off

Fresh flat leaf parsley, to garnish

1 lemon, cut into wedges

METHOD

Preheat the oven to 170°c. Trim the shoots and base off each fennel bulb, then halve and slice them, reserving any feathery fronds for a garnish. Rinse and drain the beans, tip them into a wide casserole, then add the sliced fennel in a layer on top.

Skin, deseed and roughly chop the tomatoes (see the Tuna Tartare recipe on page 128 for instructions), then add them to the casserole with the bay leaves, rosemary, garlic and saffron, plus any soaking liquid. Lastly, add the vermouth, vegetable stock and olive oil. Cover with a lid and cook in the preheated oven for 1 hour.

Remove the dish from the oven and carefully drain the liquid from the stew into a pan. Add the crème fraîche to this sauce and simmer until slightly reduced. Mix the cornflour with a little cold water, then stir this paste into the sauce to thicken it. Season well with salt and pepper, then pour the sauce back over the cooked vegetables and beans.

Lightly season the cod and pan fry in a little olive oil on one side for colour before arranging on top of the stew fried side uppermost. Return to the oven and cook uncovered for 10 minutes, or until the cod is done. Sprinkle generously with chopped parsley and fennel fronds before serving with the lemon wedges and plenty of ciabatta.

WINE NOTES

Here we have a classic Italian dish, including some wonderful fish. The Gavi region, some 70 or 80 kilometres north of Genoa on the Ligurian coast, is the home of some wonderful white wines. They use a local grape called Cortese which produces a clean, crisp, sharp wine that's perfect with fish. It's down to how much you want to pay; Cortese di Gavi will be the most expensive, but please experiment with wines from this region as they're fabulous!

CHILLED LEMON AND ALMOND SOUP

This is a delicious and fragrant starter for a hot summer's day. This soup can also be served hot, but take care not to boil it when reheating.

Preparation time: 25 minutes | Cooking time: 20 minutes | Makes 1 litre

INGREDIENTS

60g butter

2 medium-size onions

60g ground almonds

1 lemon

1 bay leaf

Pinch of ground mace

750ml light chicken stock

100-150ml double cream

Salt and white pepper, to taste

Flaked almonds, toasted

Chive flowers, to garnish

METHOD

Melt the butter in a pan while you peel and dice the onions. Stir them into the butter and cook with the lid on the pan until soft but not coloured, then add the ground almonds. Peel the zest off the lemon using a potato peeler, add this to the pan, then squeeze in the lemon juice and add the bay leaf, mace and chicken stock.

Bring to the boil and simmer for about 20 minutes. Remove the bay leaf and lemon zest, then liquidise thoroughly with a stick blender; it's important that the soup has a smooth and creamy texture. Leave to cool before stirring in your preferred quantity of cream, depending on the richness you wish to achieve. Season the soup with salt and white pepper, then refrigerate.

This rich soup is best served chilled in small portions of 150ml. Ideally, use small pots or bowls, even coffee cans or teacups, and garnish with flaked almonds which have been toasted in a hot oven and a few small chive flowers.

Serve with olive bread or a Mediterranean loaf and a saucer of extra virgin olive oil on the side.

WINE NOTES

Lemons and almonds couldn't be more Spanish, but soup is notoriously difficult to find a match for. However, we have two choices for you: how about a gloriously dry Fino Sherry, or a stone-cold glass of Verdejo, preferably from Rueda? Both of these choices will balance well with the citric acidity of the lemon. When in Spain… you know!

SPANISH MEATBALLS WITH TOMATO SAUCE

A foolproof recipe for informal lunch parties when entertaining friends.
This dish is lovely served with rice and a fresh salad, or patatas bravas and grilled
padron peppers for a tapas style meal. Our suggested dessert for this menu
is Marmalade Ice Cream (see page 54).

Preparation time: 40 minutes | Cooking time: 50 minutes | Serves 6

INGREDIENTS

For the tomato sauce

1 large onion

2 cloves of garlic

2 tablespoons oil

175ml white wine

1 x 400g tin of chopped tomatoes

1 dessertspoon tomato purée

200ml water

1 teaspoon sugar

150ml crème fraîche

For the meatballs

60g fresh breadcrumbs

90ml milk

1 egg, beaten

60g Manchego cheese, grated

1 teaspoon smoked paprika

1 tablespoon chopped fresh parsley

500g lean minced beef

500g lean minced pork

1½ teaspoons salt

Black pepper, to taste

METHOD

For the tomato sauce

Peel and finely dice the onion and crush the garlic. Heat the oil in a casserole dish, add the onion and garlic, then cook until soft, taking care not to let them burn. Add the wine and bring to the boil to cook off the alcohol. Stir in the chopped tomatoes, tomato purée and water. Season the sauce with salt and black pepper to taste, stir in the sugar, then simmer gently for 10 minutes. Remove the pan from the heat and stir in the crème fraîche.

For the meatballs

Preheat the oven to 180°c. Put the fresh breadcrumbs into a large bowl, pour in the milk and allow them to soak before adding the beaten egg, grated cheese, smoked paprika and parsley. Mix well, then add the beef and pork mince. Combine all the ingredients thoroughly, then season with the salt and pepper.

Using damp hands, shape the mince mixture into meatballs the size of golf balls. You should be able to make 40 to 50. Gently reheat the tomato sauce and carefully add the meatballs all at once. Though tempting, do not stir as the meatballs will disintegrate.

Once the meatballs are in the sauce, bring it to a gentle simmer and swirl the casserole dish to coat all the meatballs with sauce. Cover and transfer to the preheated oven to cook for about 30 minutes. After this time the meatballs should be firm, so stir gently and taste to check the seasoning. Return the casserole to the oven uncovered and cook for a further 10 minutes, allowing the sauce to thicken slightly.

Serve the meatballs in tomato sauce over long grain rice with a dressed salad of crisp leaves, cucumber, sliced red onion, green peppers, tomatoes, green olives and chopped parsley.

WINE NOTES

Spain grows huge amounts of Tempranillo, a black grape variety. It's the main ingredient in Rioja and Navarra, and indeed in Ribera del Duero. There is a reason for this: they make such a wonderful job of it! My suggestion is to look further than Rioja and try a Crianza from Cigales or Navarra, or search out something from Campo de Borja. Get experimental, it's worth it!

THAI FISHCAKES WITH CUCUMBER SALAD

We always love our Thai-themed days at Food & Company, led by the charming Jah, who is originally from Thailand. We now know that Thai food is as much about the culture as the vibrant and distinct flavours.

Preparation time: 20 minutes | Cooking time: 15 minutes | Serves 6

INGREDIENTS

For the fishcakes

500g salmon fillets

2 kaffir lime leaves

½ lime

60g green beans

3 spring onions

Small bunch of fresh coriander

1 teaspoon finely grated fresh ginger

2 teaspoons Thai red curry paste

1 dessertspoon fish sauce

Black pepper, to taste

For the cucumber salad

½ small red onion

2 tablespoons mirin

2 teaspoons caster sugar

1 whole cucumber

1 medium-hot red chilli

1 tablespoon chopped fresh mint

METHOD

For the fishcakes

Preheat the oven to 180°c. Remove any skin or bones from the salmon, then mince, blend or finely chop the fillets, leaving some texture. Put the salmon into a large bowl.

Cut the centre stems out of the kaffir leaves, discard these and shred the leaves finely. Zest the lime, finely slice the green beans and spring onions, chop the coriander (including the soft stalks) and add all these ingredients to the bowl of salmon. Mix well, then stir in the grated ginger, red curry paste, fish sauce and black pepper.

Divide the fishcake mixture into six portions, dampen your hands and then shape each portion into a fishcake. Flatten them slightly and place on a lined baking tray.

Cook the fishcakes in the preheated oven for about 10 to 12 minutes, until the salmon turns opaque and is firm. There's no need to turn the fishcakes over during cooking.

For the cucumber salad

Thinly slice the onion and place in a small pan with the mirin and sugar. Heat the mixture for 3 to 5 minutes, then leave it to cool.

Meanwhile, peel the cucumber and halve it lengthways. Use the tip of a teaspoon to scrape out the seeds, then either finely slice the cucumber, or lay it flat on a board and use a potato peeler to create ribbons. Put these into a small bowl.

Finely dice the red chilli, only using half or a milder one if you prefer less heat. Just before serving, drain off and squeeze any excess liquid from the cucumber and stir in the diced red chilli and chopped mint. Pour over the onion dressing and stir gently to combine.

WINE NOTES

Well here is a country with no real wine industry, so our regional choice won't work! In this case, I would be looking for an off-dry Riesling, probably from Germany or Austria, but we have found some wonderful examples from New Zealand too. The cucumber salad will shout at a very dry wine so beware; even if you don't really enjoy the sweeter styles, you may be surprised.

THAI GREEN CHICKEN CURRY

Delicate and fragrant, this is one of the most popular of all Thai dishes. It's worth going the extra mile and making the paste from scratch; the flavour is far superior to shop-bought versions. Our suggested dessert for this menu is Honey Poached Pineapple with Passionfruit Cream (see page 96).

Preparation time: 30 minutes | Cooking time: 30 minutes | Serves 6

INGREDIENTS

For the paste

1 teaspoon cumin seeds

2 teaspoons each coriander seeds and black peppercorns

2 lemongrass stalks

2 kaffir lime leaves

15 small green chillies, deseeded

1 small shallot, sliced

4 cloves of garlic, sliced

30g galangal or root ginger, grated

2 limes, zested

30g fresh coriander

1 tablespoon fish sauce

4 tablespoons vegetable oil

1 teaspoon salt

For the curry

1 tablespoon vegetable oil

2 tablespoons green curry paste

2 kaffir lime leaves

2 x 400ml tins of rich coconut milk

1 dessertspoon light brown sugar

1 tablespoon fish sauce

150ml chicken stock

360g mixed vegetables (carrot, mangetout and broccoli work well)

1.2kg skinned, boned chicken breast

2 teaspoons cornflour

30g fresh coriander leaves, chopped

METHOD

For the paste

This recipe makes 200g but it freezes well to be used in future curries. Toast the cumin and coriander seeds in a dry frying pan, then grind them to a fine powder with the black peppercorns in a mortar and pestle. Slice up the lower third of the lemongrass stalks (discarding the rest) and remove the centre stem of the lime leaves, shredding the rest.

Put all the ingredients except the ground spices into a tall vessel that will fit a stick blender in and blitz everything to a paste. This process takes a few moments, so be patient. Add the ground spices to the paste and blitz again. Store the curry paste in a lidded glass jar in the fridge, or freeze in portions of 2 tablespoons to use at another time.

For the curry

Put the oil in a wok on a medium heat. Add the curry paste and kaffir lime leaves, stir and cook for 1 minute until fragrant. Pour in the coconut milk, bring to the boil and simmer for 3 minutes. Stir in the brown sugar and fish sauce, then continue to simmer over a medium heat for 10 minutes. Meanwhile, prepare the vegetables: cut the carrots into thin matchsticks, halve the mangetout and break the broccoli into small florets. Thinly slice the chicken, cutting across the breast diagonally, and set to one side. Add the stock to the curry sauce and bring to a simmer.

Add the chicken to the curry in one batch and stir through, then cook on for 5 minutes. Blend the cornflour with a little cold water and add this paste to the curry, which should thicken the sauce slightly. Lastly, add the prepared vegetables and cook very briefly to retain their crisp texture. Stir in the chopped coriander before serving the curry with steamed Thai jasmine rice and prawn crackers.

WINE NOTES

Thai Green Curry is one of our favourite dishes, and a chance to bring out a big white wine. We're thinking a Chenin Blanc from South Africa will fit the bill here. Specifically, look for "Old Vines" written on the label. This will reward you with a deeper and more pronounced flavour. You could even go with an oaky Chardonnay, or a Californian Viognier.

CALIFORNIA DREAMING

Margaret and Richard travel to California on a regular basis, where their eldest son Thomas lives with his wonderful wife Catarina, who has Portuguese roots. Her kitchen is a very special place, as she is a great home cook who uses quality ingredients. We always have plenty of recipes to share and some of the dishes end up being a fusion of Cumbrian, Portuguese and Californian influences. Catarina especially loves to spoil the children with their favourite dishes on special occasions, be it birthdays, Thanksgiving or Christmas when Samantha, Nick and Sawyer along with the twins, Jack and Francesca, are gathered around the family table.

They live in San Jose on the south side of San Francisco Bay, in the centre of a state which is referred to as the breadbasket of America thanks to the abundance of fresh produce. An early morning weekend trip to the local farmers' market is a highlight for everyone, and we've tried to showcase some of the produce you can find there in this chapter. Artichokes, almonds, walnuts, avocados, lemons, blueberries and tomatoes ripened in the Californian sunshine are some of the highlights, not forgetting the crusty sourdough bread.

Another welcome addition to our Californian trips are the vineyards, including a particular favourite that produces excellent chardonnays and pinot noir. After the long journey to San Jose, we are always met with a freshly brewed pot of tea, swiftly followed by a glass of Californian wine. Catarina also treats us to appetizers and then a delicious home cooked supper. Tom often plays Fleetwood Mac and we reminisce about journeys in the Volvo packed to the rafters after a catering event back home!

We have some lovely memories of toasting marshmallows round a fire on the beach, picnics, barbecues and making Grandma's Shortbread with the grandchildren. The American family do enjoy a few specialities from the UK; we are always instructed to bring golden syrup, breakfast tea and their favourite chocolate with us! The warm and sunny weather certainly helps create a very laid back lifestyle, and it's always a pleasure to visit this special place.

"Walking on sunshine"

MEXICAN BAKED EGGS

Eggs are always at the heart of a good breakfast in America. This recipe is a reminder of the time Richard and Margaret joined the queue to have brunch at the famous Mama's on Washington Square in San Francisco, where all sorts of eggs were on the menu.

Preparation time: 20 minutes | Cooking time: 8 minutes | Serves 2

INGREDIENTS

1 teaspoon fennel seeds

4 sundried tomatoes in oil from a jar, roughly chopped

100g chorizo, chopped or sliced

1-2 cloves of garlic, finely chopped (optional)

4 small waxy potatoes, cooked and diced

1 medium-size red jalapeño chilli, deseeded and finely chopped

1 heaped teaspoon tomato purée

3 tablespoons hot water

2 large fresh free-range eggs

Salt and black pepper, to taste

Fresh coriander or chives, to garnish

METHOD

Preheat the oven to 180°c. Toast the fennel seeds in a dry frying pan, then grind them to a powder using a pestle and mortar.

Heat a little oil from the jar of sundried tomatoes in the frying pan. Add the chorizo, cook for a few minutes, then add the garlic, potatoes and sundried tomatoes. Cook for a few more minutes before adding the ground fennel and chopped chilli, allowing the flavours to come together.

Mix the tomato purée with the hot water and add this carefully to the pan, as it will steam and spit. Cook until most of the liquid has evaporated, then crack the eggs on top and season with salt and black pepper to taste.

Transfer the frying pan to the preheated oven and bake the eggs for about 8 minutes until the white is just set and the yolk is still wobbly. It's very easy to overcook them so watch carefully. You could also cook this on the top of the stove by covering the pan with a lid.

To serve, sprinkle the baked eggs with chopped fresh herbs of your choice. A great addition on the side is smashed avocado and toasted sourdough bread.

HINTS & TIPS
If you prefer lots of spice, try using a hot variety of chorizo.

CARROT & CORIANDER MUFFINS

Muffins are an ubiquitous American food, but these are far removed from the chocolate version we know and love. We enjoy making these in small terracotta pots; they always make a good impression and taste good too.

Preparation time: 20 minutes | Cooking time: 20 minutes | Makes 12 small muffins

INGREDIENTS

2 teaspoons coriander seeds

240g carrots

60g Demerara sugar

2 large eggs

175ml vegetable oil

60g raisins

60g walnuts, chopped

½ teaspoon ground cumin

½ teaspoon ground cinnamon

½ teaspoon salt

1 teaspoon bicarbonate of soda

210g plain flour

METHOD

Preheat the oven to 180°c. Line 12 mini terracotta pots with a square of baking paper in each, or line a muffin tin with paper cases. In a dry frying pan, toast the coriander seeds and then grind them to a powder in a mortar and pestle. Peel and grate the carrots.

In a large bowl, combine the Demerara sugar, eggs and oil by whisking or beating until smooth. Stir in the grated carrot, raisins, walnuts, spices, salt and bicarbonate of soda. Fold in the sifted flour until everything is just mixed.

Divide the mixture between the lined pots or paper cases, then bake in the preheated oven for about 20 minutes. These muffins are delicious with butter and can also be served with soup.

HINTS & TIPS

The muffin tin can also act as a tray when using terracotta pots, to hold them in place and make them easier to move around when hot.

L.A. FONDUE

The young set just adore this Californian recipe and will find any excuse to have it at a party! It's very simple to make; just pop into the oven and wait. The hot cheese dip is passed from person to person until the last tiny bit has been scraped from inside the bread.

Preparation time: 20 minutes | Cooking time: 1 hour | Serves a crowd

INGREDIENTS

1 medium-size round crusty loaf

1 bunch of spring onions

3 cloves of garlic

30g butter

360g cheddar cheese, grated

300ml soured cream

Salt and ground black pepper, to taste

1 small jar of artichokes, drained and roughly chopped

180g cream cheese (such as Philadelphia)

4 red dessert apples, to serve

METHOD

Preheat the oven to 180°c. Cut a generous lid off the crusty loaf and use your hands to pull out the insides of the bread. Be careful not to make any holes in the bread shell. The excess bread can be made into breadcrumbs and frozen for use in other recipes.

Slice the spring onions and finely chop the garlic, then sauté them in a pan with the butter until soft and take off the heat.

In a large bowl, combine the grated cheddar and soured cream, then stir in the spring onion and garlic mixture. Season to taste with salt and pepper. Mix in the artichokes and carefully fold through teaspoons of the cream cheese, leaving them intact to create pockets of creaminess.

Put the cheese mixture into the bread shell and place it on a baking sheet. Bake the fondue for 50 minutes in the preheated oven without the lid on the bread. Remove from the oven and put the lid on top of the loaf, then place back in the oven to bake for the remaining 10 minutes.

To serve, transfer the fondue straight from the oven to a large serving dish or tray and surround it with freshly cut slices of apple and bite-size pieces of the bread lid for dunking into the fondue.

HINTS & TIPS

Sticks of celery or breadsticks are also great for dipping in this fondue. The next day, you can cut the empty bread shell into small pieces and brown them in a hot oven to make wonderful cheesy bites.

TUNA TARTARE

It is essential to use the freshest tuna available for this recipe. The combination of top quality ingredients makes this a fresh and delicious starter for a day filled with sunshine. Best served chilled, straight from the fridge with a glass of Californian white wine.

Preparation time: 15 minutes, plus 30 minutes chilling time | Serves 6 as a starter

INGREDIENTS

1 level tablespoon soured cream

1 teaspoon fish sauce

½ lemon, zested and juiced

2 tablespoons olive oil

3 spring onions, finely sliced

1 teaspoon capers, drained and chopped

1 tablespoon chopped fresh coriander

½ clove of garlic, crushed

1 tomato, skinned and deseeded (see method)

200g fresh tuna steak

1 avocado

Black pepper, to taste

Rocket and radishes, to garnish

METHOD

Combine the soured cream, fish sauce, lemon zest, lemon juice and olive oil in a bowl. Gently stir through the spring onions, capers, coriander and garlic.

Cut both the tomato flesh and tuna into a fine dice and add them to the dressing, mixing everything together gently. Finally, peel and dice the avocado to a similar size, add to the bowl, season with black pepper and combine.

Divide the mixture between 6 food presentation rings (about 5cm in diameter) and carefully press the tartare down to firm. If you don't have any food presentation rings, just use a plain scone cutter. Fill the mould, gently press down on the tartare, carefully remove the cutter and repeat. Cover and chill for at least 30 minutes before turning out onto plates. Serve with some dressed rocket leaves and garnish with finely sliced radish. Toasted sourdough is great alongside the tartare too.

To skin a fresh tomato

First fill a bowl with cold water and add several ice cubes. Using a paring knife, score the tomato into quarters by making a shallow incision from the stalk end all the way around to meet itself, and then repeat this in the other direction. Put the tomato into a heatproof bowl, cover with boiling water until completely submerged, leave in the water for 1 minute, then use a slotted spoon to transfer the tomato into the bowl of iced water. Let it stand for a while until cool. The tomato skin will now peel off in quarters very easily. If the tomato is underripe and has a thicker skin, you may need to leave it in the boiling water for longer. Once peeled, quarter the tomato, remove the core and discard any seeds using your hands. Cut the tomato flesh into the required size.

BEEF CHILLI

A super recipe for this classic dish, using diced brisket which gives the chilli great texture. With our secret ingredient of coffee, you'll be knocked out by the intense flavours which will really develop if made a day ahead. If you like it hot just add more spice.

Preparation time: 25 minutes | Cooking time: 1 hour 30 minutes | Serves 6

INGREDIENTS

1kg rolled brisket of beef

2 tablespoons vegetable oil

2 onions, peeled and chopped

3 cloves of garlic, crushed

1 tablespoon cumin seeds

1 teaspoon each of chilli powder, cayenne pepper, paprika and salt

1 bay leaf

1 green pepper, finely diced

1 x 400g tin of chopped tomatoes

120ml strong coffee

1 x 400g tin of red kidney beans

Small bunch of basil, shredded

METHOD

Preheat the oven to 150°c. Dice the brisket into 1cm cubes and heat the oil in a large casserole. Fry the beef in a single batch until sealed all over, then add the onion and garlic and cook on.

Toast the cumin seeds in a dry frying pan, then grind them to a powder using a pestle and mortar. Add the cumin to the casserole along with the chilli powder, cayenne pepper and paprika, then cook the spices for a minute or two. Finally, add the salt, bay leaf, green pepper and tinned tomatoes. Half fill the tomato tin with water, swirl it around to rinse the tin, then add this to the casserole as well. Stir and bring to a simmer, cover with a close-fitting lid and cook in the preheated oven for 45 minutes.

Remove the chilli from the oven, stir in the coffee, then cook in the oven for a further 45 minutes. Towards the end of the cooking time, add the drained and rinsed kidney beans. Just before serving, stir in the shredded basil. Serve the chilli in bowls, wraps or bread rolls with some finely shredded crisp lettuce, grated cheese, soured cream and guacamole. Don't forget the tortilla chips!

GUACAMOLE

This delicious dip is easy to make and tastes so much better than the supermarket versions: well worth the effort. It's best made and eaten on the same day.

Preparation time: 10 minutes | Makes 1 bowl

INGREDIENTS

1 tomato, skinned and deseeded

¼ small red onion, grated

1 lime, zested and juiced

½ clove of garlic, crushed

1 red chilli, deseeded, finely diced

Fresh coriander, chopped

2 ripe avocados

Salt and black pepper, to taste

Pinch of caster sugar (optional)

METHOD

Finely dice the tomato flesh (see method on page 128) and combine this with the grated onion, lime zest and juice, crushed garlic and diced chilli in a bowl. Stir well, then add the chopped coriander.

Cut the avocados in half, remove the stones, scoop the flesh out of the skins and mash it with a fork. Add the mashed avocado to the bowl and mix well. Season the guacamole to taste - a little pinch of sugar may transform it - and serve as soon as possible with the bean or beef chilli.

BEAN CHILLI

Catarina makes this every winter when the family visit Tahoe with friends; it is a must after a day's skiing. We like to serve this store cupboard recipe at barbecues: it's easy, no fuss and caters for those who prefer not to eat meat... the trouble is, everyone digs in!

Preparation time: 25 minutes | Cooking time: 40 minutes | Serves 10

INGREDIENTS

2 medium-size onions

500g carrots

2 cloves of garlic

2 tablespoons vegetable oil

1 tablespoon cumin seeds

2 tablespoons mild chilli powder

1 teaspoon cayenne pepper

2 x 415g tins of baked beans in tomato sauce

2 x 420g tins of borlotti beans

1 x 420g tin of red kidney beans

2 x 420g tins of chopped tomatoes

450ml water

1 tablespoon vegetable stock powder or 1 stock cube

300g frozen sweetcorn

Salt and ground black pepper, to taste

1 dessertspoon cornflour

Fresh coriander, chopped

METHOD

Peel the onions, carrots and garlic. Chop roughly and then use a food processor to blitz them into a very fine dice. Heat the oil in a large pan, add the vegetables and cook until they are beginning to soften.

Meanwhile, toast the cumin seeds in a dry pan, then grind them to a powder using a pestle and mortar. Add the cumin to the vegetables along with the chilli powder and cayenne (reducing the latter to half a teaspoon if you don't like too much heat). Cook the spices for a few moments before adding the baked beans. Stir well.

Drain and rinse the rest of the beans, then add them to the pan with the tinned tomatoes, water and stock powder. Allow the liquid to reach simmering point before adding the sweetcorn, then simmer gently for 20 minutes, stirring occasionally. Lastly, check the seasoning and thicken the sauce by blending the cornflour with a little cold water and stirring this paste into the chilli.

To serve, top the chilli with chopped coriander and serve with plain boiled rice, guacamole (see page 130), soured cream and grated cheese.

HINTS & TIPS

This is a naturally gluten-free recipe.

It's great with baked potatoes for an easy weeknight dinner or warming up a crowd.

Our recipe makes a large quantity but freezes brilliantly, or you could halve the ingredients.

STUFFED AUBERGINE ROLLS
WITH TOMATO SAUCE

A lovely 'cook now, eat later' dish for a leisurely lunch. It's also a great main course dish to serve at a dinner party for vegetarian guests alongside meat eaters. The aubergine rolls go beautifully with vegetables and even have their own sauce. Perfect.

Preparation time: 40 minutes | Cooking time: 1 hour | Serves 6

INGREDIENTS

2 medium-size aubergines

120g Lancashire cheese

60g pine nuts

60g raisins

45g fresh breadcrumbs

30g parmesan, freshly grated

1 clove of garlic

½ teaspoon salt

Black pepper, to taste

1 egg

1 tablespoon olive oil

30g fresh basil

500g passata

1 ball of buffalo mozzarella, sliced

METHOD

Preheat the oven to 160°c. Remove the stalks from the aubergines and slice each one lengthways into at least 6 pieces. Heat some oil in a griddle pan or a frying pan and shallow fry the aubergine slices in batches. You may need extra oil, but be careful not to add too much as the aubergines will absorb it. Turn the slices over, season lightly with salt and black pepper, continue cooking until tender, then transfer to a plate lined with kitchen roll and leave to cool.

Meanwhile, make the filling. Crumble the Lancashire cheese into a large bowl, then add the pine nuts, raisins, fresh breadcrumbs and grated parmesan. Crush the garlic with the salt and stir gently into the mixture. Season to taste with black pepper, then bring the filling together by adding the beaten egg and olive oil. Shred most of the basil into the bowl, leaving a few leaves whole for garnishing the finished dish.

Lay the aubergine slices on a clean surface and divide the filling between them. Roll up from bottom to top, gently placing each roll side by side in an ovenproof dish as you go. When all the aubergine rolls are ready, pour over the passata and cook in the preheated oven for 40 minutes. Top the baked rolls with the sliced mozzarella and cook for a final 5 minutes to melt the cheese. Just before serving, sprinkle the dish with the remaining fresh basil.

HINTS & TIPS
You could make this recipe in individual portions using mini gratin dishes.
It also freezes very well when assembled.

ROASTED SWEET POTATO SALAD

This is a very simple and refreshing change from English potato salad, which looks very attractive served on a platter. The recipe uses some fantastic American ingredients such as golden sultanas, which are a great buy if you are able to source them.

Preparation time: 30 minutes | Cooking time: 30 minutes | Serves 8

INGREDIENTS

1kg sweet potatoes

60g whole almonds, skins on

60g golden sultanas

½ bunch of spring onions, chopped

Generous handful each of chopped fresh coriander or parsley and rocket

For the dressing

1 tablespoon olive oil

½ tablespoon each of maple syrup and sherry vinegar

¼ small orange, zested and juiced

¼ teaspoon ground cinnamon

METHOD

Preheat the oven to 180°c. Peel the sweet potatoes and slice them evenly. Place in a roasting tin, drizzle with olive oil and season with salt and black pepper. Use your hands to mix well so they are coated in the oil and seasoning. Roast the sweet potatoes in the preheated oven for about 30 minutes, turning them halfway through, then set aside.

Meanwhile, toast the almonds in a hot dry frying pan. Let them cool before chopping roughly. To make the dressing, put all of the ingredients into a lidded jar and shake well. Season to taste with salt and pepper, then stir in some chilli jam and grated fresh ginger to taste if you like.

To serve, transfer the sweet potatoes into a bowl and combine them with the almonds, sultanas, spring onions and fresh herbs. Cover the base of a wide serving platter with rocket leaves, turn out the sweet potato salad on top and then drizzle over the dressing.

QUINOA & FETA SALAD

Catarina often makes this refreshing and nourishing salad to take with them when going on RV trips or a beach picnic. For a work lunch, make a 'Dig Deep Salad' by layering up this quinoa salad in a clear plastic box with roasted red peppers, thinly sliced tomatoes and salad leaves on top. Add a lid and off you go!

Preparation time: 15 minutes | Cooking time: 10 minutes | Serves 8

INGREDIENTS

3 sticks of celery

2 tablespoons olive oil

250g pre-cooked quinoa

½ cucumber

3 spring onions, chopped

60g dried cranberries

1 lime, zested and juiced

Fresh mint, chopped

90g feta cheese

Black pepper, to taste

METHOD

Finely chop the celery and cook gently in a pan with the olive oil until al dente. Turn out into a large bowl and leave to cool. Meanwhile, peel and deseed the cucumber then chop into bite-size pieces.

Add the quinoa to the celery along with the spring onions, cucumber and cranberries. Mix well, then stir in the lime zest, lime juice and fresh mint. Finally, crumble in the feta cheese. Season with black pepper but not with salt, because feta cheese is already salty.

Serve the salad in an attractive bowl. This is especially delicious served alongside chicken dishes. Black beans can be substituted for the feta cheese if you like.

LEMON MERINGUE ROULADE

This is a recipe that Margaret has shared with Catarina and she loves to make it when visiting the family across the pond. When they need a lemon, they just pick one from the tree in the garden! Their roulade is served semi-frozen as it is so refreshing when the sun is beating down.

Preparation time: 30 minutes | Cooking time: 30 minutes | Serves 8

INGREDIENTS

3 egg whites

180g caster sugar, sifted

1 lemon, zested and juiced

180g lemon curd

300ml double cream

METHOD

Preheat the oven to 150°c and line a large, flat baking tray with baking paper. In a clean bowl, whisk the egg whites using an electric handheld whisk until they are stiff and beginning to look dry. Add the caster sugar gradually and continue to whisk until the mixture is thick and glossy.

Spread the meringue mixture onto the lined tray in a square, about 27cm on each side.

Bake the meringue in the preheated oven for 30 minutes. It should have a firm crust on the top and be lightly coloured, with a marshmallow-like centre. Before you take the meringue out of the oven, have a piece of baking paper larger than your meringue and a cooling rack at the ready. Put the paper on top of the meringue, followed by the upturned cooling rack. Carefully flip the whole thing over, allowing the baking tray and paper to be removed. The flat underside of the meringue is now facing upwards. Leave it to cool like this on the wire rack.

In a small bowl, combine the lemon zest and juice with the curd, mixing until smooth. Whip the cream until soft peaks begin to form, then add the curd mixture to the cream and whip a little further until thick. Place the cold meringue, still on the baking paper, onto a flat surface and spread it with the lemon cream.

Score a line about 2cm in along one edge to assist you with rolling the meringue. Use the baking paper to roll the meringue and filling to form a Swiss roll. Wrap the paper tightly around the roulade and tuck or fold the ends in to help retain the shape. Chill or freeze until required.

Serve the roulade straight from the fridge (chilled or defrosted). Unwrap the paper, place the roulade on a suitable serving plate and dust with icing sugar. Delicious served with fresh fruit.

BAKED BLUEBERRY CHEESECAKE

This is easy to make, yet looks spectacular. You can use homemade or shop-bought sponges for the base of this great American dessert, which makes a pleasant change from the usual Graham crackers.

Preparation time: 35 minutes | Cooking time: 35 minutes | Serves 10

INGREDIENTS

For the cheesecake

4 trifle sponges or a 1cm deep sponge layer

340g cream cheese

45g caster sugar

1 teaspoon vanilla extract

2 whole eggs, beaten

1 tablespoon lemon juice

150ml double cream

125g blueberries

For the topping

125g blueberries

30g sugar

60ml water

1 cinnamon stick

1 teaspoon cornflour

METHOD

For the cheesecake

Preheat the oven to 180°c while you grease and line the bottom and sides of a 20 to 23cm loose-bottomed springform cake tin with butter and baking paper. Cut the trifle sponges in half horizontally and make a layer of them in the bottom of the tin, cut side uppermost.

In a bowl, beat together the cream cheese, sugar and vanilla extract until well combined and fluffy in appearance. Gently add the beaten eggs, followed by the lemon juice, and mix well.

Using an electric handheld whisk, lightly whip the cream, then fold it into the cream cheese mixture. Stir in the blueberries and scrape the mixture into the prepared tin on top of the sponge layer. Tap the tin gently on a flat surface to level the surface of the filling.

Bake the cheesecake in the preheated oven for about 35 minutes. The cheesecake should have a wobble but be set. Leave to cool in the tin, then chill in the fridge.

For the topping

Put the blueberries, sugar, water and cinnamon stick into a pan and simmer gently until the berries have burst. Blend the cornflour with a little cold water, add the paste to the pan and stir until the sauce thickens. Leave it to cool before adding to the cheesecake.

To serve

Remove the chilled cheesecake from the tin, discard the lining and place on a serving dish, ideally a flat gateau plate. Spoon the cooled blueberry sauce over the top.

HINTS & TIPS

A ready-made sponge flan case works well, as an alternative to trifle sponges, but can be tricky to source. The blueberry topping for this cheesecake would also work very well served with the Lemon Meringue Roulade on page 138.

BITE-SIZE & DELICIOUS

Over the last 30 years, we have catered for hundreds of parties up and down the county for the great and the good which has taught us many things, not least that canapés are like the grease on the wheels of a good party. Of course, they have to be delicious, otherwise you have a talking point for the wrong reasons, but done properly they can ensure the occasion gets off to a good start and flows smoothly onwards. These recipes are the pick of the bunch, with a couple of drinks thrown in to give you all the foundations for a great party.

Small bites that need to look good can be somewhat fiddly and time-consuming, but they do create a 'wow factor' for your guests. Choose your selection carefully and make sure flavours and textures are balanced, without too much pastry and bread. You can always stretch them out with shop-bought elements such as olives and posh crisps. We also advise keeping them bite-size, not serving them scorching hot to avoid burnt fingers and tongues, providing napkins, and steering well clear of slippery or heavy platters and trays to carry them on. The last thing you need is hours of careful cooking cascading to the floor! We love to garnish our platters and trays with stems of flowers, freshly picked from the garden if possible, for extra flourish.

However, canapés aren't just for occasions and make a brilliant informal option for the beginning of a meal instead of sitting down to a plated starter. Bring them into everyday life and serve to friends and family too; Joan's daughter Sally and her partner Jamie absolutely love the mango salsa and sticky sausages, which are both easy to make.

Our ultimate canapé is the Solway Shrimp Tart, which was enjoyed in the early days by Jennifer Paterson of Two Fat Ladies fame; she was at a party we were catering for and absolutely loved them. Jennifer wrote about the occasion afterwards in her cookery column for The Oldie magazine, describing "a lunch party held in Cumberland, catered for by charming girls in black and white with sweet faces, perfect manners and great expertise" and that was us!

"Just one more!"

CHEESY COCKTAIL BISCUITS

Delicious, crumbly and full of flavour. These are great to pull out of the freezer when you have impromptu guests. They'll think you've gone to so much trouble!

Preparation time: 25 minutes, plus 20 minutes chilling | Cooking time: 12-15 minutes | Makes 64

INGREDIENTS

120g cheese (mature cheddar or a mixture of hard cheeses)

120g plain flour

Pinch of salt

110g butter, cut into small pieces

Sesame seeds

1 egg, beaten

Flaked almonds (optional)

METHOD

Grate the cheese, sift the flour and salt into a bowl and then rub in the butter. Add the cheese and mix together to form a firm dough. Cut the dough in half and then cut one piece in half again. Roll the smaller pieces into two sausages about 20cm long. Sprinkle a generous amount of sesame seeds onto the table then roll the dough through them until coated. Put the logs and the spare piece of dough on a tray and chill for 20 minutes.

Preheat the oven to 180°c. Roll out the remaining piece of dough with a rolling pin to a 16 by 16cm square. Cut this into 16 squares, and then cut each square into two triangles. Lightly egg wash the tops using the beaten egg and then sprinkle with flaked almonds if using. Place the triangular biscuits onto a tray lined with baking paper and set to one side.

Cut each of the sesame seeded rolls into 16 biscuits and place these on another lined baking tray. Bake both trays of biscuits in the preheated oven for about 10 to 15 minutes until golden. Cool on a wire rack and store in an airtight container.

SALTED OAT BISCUITS

These crisp biscuits can showcase a variety of savoury toppings, whether they are homemade or shop-bought. They look gorgeous if you use a mix-and-match selection on the same platter.

Preparation time: 15 minutes | Cooking time: 10-12 minutes | Makes 75

INGREDIENTS

120g plain flour

120g rolled oats

45g caster sugar

¼ teaspoon bicarbonate of soda

Pinch of salt

45g butter

45g lard

3 tablespoons milk

METHOD

Preheat the oven to 180°c. Put all the dry ingredients into a large bowl and mix together. Cut the fats into small pieces and add to the dry ingredients, then rub them in to get a breadcrumb-like consistency before adding the milk to form a dough. Turn out the dough onto a floured board and cut in half. Using a rolling pin, roll out the first piece to the thickness of a pound coin. Use a round, plain cutter about 4cm in diameter to cut out the biscuits and place them on a lined baking tray. Add any off-cuts to the second piece of dough and repeat until all the dough is used up.

Bake the biscuits in the preheated oven for about 12 minutes or until they begin to turn golden around the edges. Sprinkle lightly with sea salt while still hot, then cool on a wire rack. Store in an airtight container or freeze until required.

CHEESE & CHILLI SCONES

Anyone who loves hot chilli will adore these scones. A savoury delight with a kick of heat lingering at the end, our cheese and chilli scones offer a substantial bite that pleases any party goer, but especially vegetarian guests.

Preparation time: 20 minutes | Cooking time: 8-10 minutes | Makes 24 x 4cm scones

INGREDIENTS

2 medium-sized red jalapeño chillies

240g self-raising flour (we use Carr's)

1 level teaspoon baking powder

½ teaspoon cayenne pepper

Pinch of salt

90g butter, cut into small pieces

120g mature cheddar cheese, grated

150ml milk

METHOD

Preheat the oven to 200°c. With care, remove and discard the seeds from the chillies. Chop them finely then leave to one side.

Sift the flour into a large bowl with the baking powder, cayenne pepper and salt. Rub the butter into the dry ingredients with your fingertips until a breadcrumb consistency is reached, then add the cheese and chopped chillies. Mix well before adding most of the milk. Stir with a round-bladed knife until a firm dough is formed.

Turn out the dough onto a floured board and knead lightly. Gently flatten the dough with a rolling pin to an even 2cm thickness. Cut out the scones using a 4cm round cutter, then reroll the leftover dough to repeat. Place the scones on a baking sheet, brush the tops with the remaining milk and bake in the preheated oven for about 8 to 10 minutes. Cool on a wire rack.

To serve

Split the scones in half and spread them with butter, pipe some cream cheese or soft goat's cheese on top, add a dab of chilli jam and garnish with a piece of fresh strawberry.

HINTS & TIPS

These can be reheated from frozen in a hot oven for 5 minutes.
Try substituting the jalapeño chillies with your favourite ingredient that goes well with cheese, such as thyme or spring onions.

CUMBERLAND SAUSAGE PINWHEELS

Shh... don't tell anyone, but these are really just posh sausage rolls! They're always a hit wherever we serve them: crisp, buttery pastry with Cumbria's famous Cumberland sausage.

Preparation time: 10 minutes | Cooking time: 15-20 minutes | Makes 40

INGREDIENTS

For the pinwheels

375g ready-rolled puff pastry

1 egg, beaten with a little milk

400g sausage meat

60g dried apricots, chopped into small pieces

For the caramelised chestnuts (optional)

15g butter

1 teaspoon sugar

60g cooked chestnuts, peeled and chopped

Pinch of salt and pepper

1 clove of garlic, finely chopped

METHOD

For the pinwheels

Preheat the oven to 175°c. Unwrap the puff pastry and leave it on the paper, dusting with a little flour if the pastry becomes sticky. Cut it in half so you have two pieces approximately 25 by 15cm. With a pastry brush, moisten the two outer edges of the pastry with the egg wash.

Spread the sausage meat evenly over both pieces of pastry so that only the egg washed edges are visible. Scatter the apricots over the sausage meat and gently press them in. Similar to a Swiss roll, roll up the pastry towards the outer edge and press on the egg washed strip to secure. Repeat the same action with the second roll.

Wrap each roll in cling film, twisting the ends tightly to keep a good shape, then chill until firm to give you neater slices. To get ahead, make and chill the rolls overnight and then cook just before serving. Unwrap and carefully cut each roll into 20 thin slices using a sharp knife and a sawing action. Place the pinwheels flat on a lined baking sheet. Brush them with egg wash before cooking in a preheated oven until golden and crisp for about 15 to 20 minutes.

Remove the cooked pinwheels from the oven and place on a wire rack to cool, then store in an airtight container. If you're not serving them straightaway, refresh in a hot oven for a few minutes and then arrange on a flat basket or plate.

For the caramelised chestnuts (optional)

Melt the butter in a small saucepan, then add the sugar and stir until dissolved. Add the chestnuts and seasoning, cook gently for a minute and then add the garlic. Continue cooking for another minute then remove the saucepan from the heat. Let the chestnuts cool before using them in the pinwheels.

HINTS & TIPS

Try substituting the chopped apricots with 2 tablespoons of honey mustard spread over the sausage meat, or use caramelised chestnuts for a delicious Christmas version.

TWO WAYS WITH CRAB TARTS

The buttered crab recipe is adapted from the personal recipe book of Elizabeth Rainbow, the Bishop of Carlisle's wife, and was served at the Feast of Two Houses, Dalemain and Rose Castle. Her collection of recipes still resides at Dalemain to this day.

Preparation time: 15 minutes, plus 2 hours chilling | Makes 30 each

INGREDIENTS

For buttered crab tarts

100g fresh white crab meat (from a deli counter or fishmonger)

1 teaspoon cider vinegar

2 teaspoons pale cream sherry or vermouth

½ level teaspoon ground cinnamon

¼ teaspoon sugar (optional)

1 hard-boiled egg

45g butter, melted

Small amount of mayonnaise

30 mini pastry cases (see page 154)

A few chives, finely chopped

Pinch of paprika

For curried crab & apple tarts

100g tinned white crab meat

2 tablespoons mayonnaise

1 teaspoon curry powder, or to taste

½ red apple

30 mini pastry cases (see page 154)

Fresh parsley, finely chopped

Pinch of paprika

METHOD

For buttered crab tarts

Put the crab meat into a bowl and combine well with the cider vinegar, sherry, cinnamon and sugar if using. Separate the yolk from the white of the hard-boiled egg and push the yolk through a sieve, then add it to the crab mixture. Do the same with the egg white but reserve it to garnish the tarts later. Finally, stir the melted butter into the crab mixture, season with salt and pepper to taste, then turn out and spread onto a plate. Chill for at least 2 hours before serving.

To assemble the tarts, pipe some mayonnaise into the base of each pastry case. Break up the chilled buttered crab with a fork and use this to fill the tarts. Garnish with the egg white and chopped chives, then sprinkle with paprika to finish.

For curried crab & apple tarts

Drain the tinned white crab meat and dab with some kitchen roll to remove any excess moisture, then break it up using a fork. Combine the mayonnaise with the teaspoon of curry powder, adding more if you want to give the mayo a mild spicy flavour. Mix them together well. Grate the red apple with the skin still on into a bowl, then squeeze gently to get rid of any excess moisture. Add the grated apple and crab meat to the mayonnaise, mix thoroughly, then chill the curried crab filling until required.

To assemble the tarts, spoon the filling into the pastry cases and garnish the tarts with some chopped parsley and a dusting of paprika to finish.

HINTS & TIPS

Do not fill the pastry cases too far in advance; the tarts are best assembled just before serving. Tinned white crab meat can be difficult to find in some supermarkets, but it's worth stocking up when you do come across it, making these quick and easy curried crab tarts great for those unexpected guests!

ENGLISH ASPARAGUS
WITH HOLLANDAISE SAUCE

A guest at Food and Company shared one of the best tips we have ever had for cooking young slender asparagus spears and it works a treat; now we want to share it with everyone! The English asparagus season is well worth waiting for, short though it is from April to June.

Preparation time: 10 minutes | Cooking time: 10 minutes | Makes 200ml of sauce

INGREDIENTS

30 raw asparagus spears (approx. 12cm)

2 free-range egg yolks, at room temperature

1 tablespoon white wine vinegar

¼ teaspoon caster sugar

¼ teaspoon salt

White pepper, to taste

2 tablespoons lemon juice

125g salted butter

METHOD

Trim the tough end of the stems off the asparagus and place them into a cafetière with the tips facing up. Cover completely with just-boiled water and use the coffee plunger to prevent the asparagus from floating. Allow to stand for 8 minutes and then drain. Immediately wrap the asparagus tightly in a clean tea towel and roll up into a bundle. Leave for 5 minutes, then serve while still warm.

Alternatively, plunge the asparagus into a pan of salted boiling water and cook for 2 to 3 minutes. After draining, submerge them in a bowl of iced water to prevent them from overcooking. Drain again and wrap in a clean tea towel. Refrigerate until required.

To make the hollandaise sauce, put the yolks, vinegar, sugar, salt and pepper into a tall vessel and blend this small quantity briefly with a stick blender. Heat the lemon juice until steaming hot, then with the blender running, pour it into the yolk mixture. Heat the butter in a small pan until it is foaming, taking care not to burn it. Add it to the yolks in a steady stream with the stick blender running until the sauce is a thick emulsion.

Serve the warm hollandaise immediately with the cooked asparagus, or leave to cool and chill until required.

ENGLISH ASPARAGUS WITH PANCETTA

Preparation time: 5 minutes | Cooking time: 10 minutes } Makes 30 pieces

INGREDIENTS

15 asparagus spears, raw and untrimmed (approx. 20cm)

Olive oil

Black pepper, to taste

15 rashers of pancetta-style bacon

METHOD

Preheat the oven to 200°c. Trim any tough ends off the asparagus stems and, using your hands, rub each spear with a little olive oil, then lightly season with black pepper. Starting at the tip, wrap the pancetta rashers along the length of the asparagus spears, overlapping the edges as you go.

Place the wrapped asparagus onto a lined baking tray, leaving space between the spears. Cook on the top shelf of the preheated oven for about 10 minutes until cooked through. Remove any excess oil and fat by resting them briefly on kitchen paper.

To serve, cut the spears in half with scissors. Allow them to cool slightly before arranging on a flat plate, with a small dish of hollandaise sauce to dip the wrapped spears into. These are also ideal for cooking on the barbecue.

TINY SOLWAY SHRIMP TARTS

J M Caterers (our previous business name) were renowned for serving Solway shrimp tarts at drinks parties. These crisp homemade pastry cases with buttery hollandaise, deliciously sweet Solway shrimps and a grating of nutmeg are perfection in one small bite, making them our number one canapé.

Preparation time: 15 minutes | Cooking time: 7 minutes | Makes 30

INGREDIENTS

For the mini parmesan pastry cases

120g plain flour

60g butter, cubed

30g parmesan, grated

1 egg, beaten

To serve

Hollandaise sauce (see page 152)

125g Solway shrimps

Grated nutmeg

METHOD

For the mini parmesan pastry cases

Preheat the oven to 180°c. Sift the flour into a large bowl, add the butter and rub into the flour until it resembles fine breadcrumbs. Stir in the parmesan, then add the egg and knead until the mixture comes together. Bring the dough into a smooth ball and turn out onto a clean work surface.

Roll out half of the pastry very thinly, until you can nearly see through it. Cut out circles using a plain cutter about 6cm in diameter and place these in a 12-hole rounded bottom patty tin. Add the pastry cut-offs to the remaining pastry and roll out once again. In total, you should be able to make 60 tart cases.

Bake the pastry cases in a preheated oven for about 7 minutes until golden in colour. Be aware that they burn very easily! When cooked and cooled on a wire rack, store in an airtight container.

To serve

Our classic method is to pipe or spoon a little hollandaise sauce in the base of the tart case and pile some Solway shrimps on top, with a grating of nutmeg to finish.

HINTS & TIPS

The tart cases will freeze extremely well; simply refresh them in a hot oven before using. We find that fish fillings work best with this parmesan pastry.

MANGO SALSA

This salsa requires minimum effort for maximum flavour. It's one of Joan's go-to recipes when the gang are coming over for a roast. A selection of no-fuss canapés is perfect for grazing when no starter is required.

Preparation time: 20 minutes, plus marinating | Cooking time: 5-10 minutes | Makes 1 bowl

INGREDIENTS

½ small red onion, finely chopped

1 dessertspoon honey

1 teaspoon chilli jam

1 dessertspoon white wine vinegar

1 lime, zested and juiced

1 medium-large ripe mango

1 tomato, skinned, deseeded and diced (for instructions see page 128)

Fresh coriander, chopped

For the toasts (optional)

3 plain bagels

Olive oil

Salt

METHOD

Mix the onion with the honey, chilli jam, vinegar, lime zest and juice in a bowl. Leave this mixture to stand for a few hours or overnight.

When you want to serve the salsa, peel the mango and finely dice the flesh. Add this to the salsa with the tomato and chopped coriander to taste. Just before serving, drain the salsa in a colander to remove any excess liquid. Put the salsa in a pretty bowl with a teaspoon so it can be spooned onto the toasts, or serve with shop-bought tortilla chips.

For the toasts (optional)

Preheat the oven to 180°c and slice each bagel into about 20 thin rounds. Put all the pieces into a large bowl and add about 6 tablespoons of olive oil to lightly massage and coat the bagels with. Arrange on two lined baking trays with an edge and cook in the preheated oven until golden. Sprinkle lightly with salt while still hot and then cool on a wire rack. Store in an airtight container until serving.

HINTS & TIPS

Use white balsamic vinegar as an alternative to white wine vinegar.
Substitute 2 ripe avocados for the mango if you like.

CHICKEN TIKKA & MINT RAITA

Would you believe that we took an Indian cookery course at our local pub? As a group of enthusiastic home cooks, we were guided through a wide repertoire of Indian cuisine. This recipe is a nod to our instructor Salim and all he taught us.

Preparation time: 15 minutes, plus up to 24 hours marinating | Cooking time: 10 minutes | Makes 60 pieces

INGREDIENTS

For the chicken tikka

1kg skinless and boneless chicken breast

½ lemon, juiced

1 teaspoon salt

2.5cm fresh ginger

6 cloves of garlic, peeled

50ml water

1 teaspoon cumin seeds

1 teaspoon coriander seeds

170ml thick natural yoghurt

1 tablespoon fenugreek leaves

1 teaspoon garam masala

1 teaspoon chilli powder

Fresh coriander, to garnish

For the mint raita

¼ of a cucumber

170g natural yoghurt

1 tablespoon chopped fresh coriander

1 tablespoon chopped fresh mint

1 tomato, skinned, deseeded and diced (see method on page 128)

½ teaspoon cumin seeds, toasted

½ lemon, juiced

Salt and ground black pepper, to taste

METHOD

For the chicken tikka

Cut the chicken breasts into bite-size pieces and spread out on a plate. Squeeze over the lemon juice and sprinkle with the salt. Leave to one side while you make the marinade.

Start by making your own ginger and garlic paste. Using a teaspoon, scrape the ginger to remove the skin. Roughly chop the ginger and place in a tall narrow jug with the peeled garlic cloves and water. Using a stick blender, blitz the mixture to a smooth purée. Store in a lidded jar in the fridge for up to one week, or freeze in an ice cube tray for further use in curries and the like.

Toast the cumin and coriander seeds in a dry frying pan, then grind to a powder using a pestle and mortar. Put the yoghurt into a large bowl with 3 teaspoons of your ginger and garlic paste, the fenugreek leaves, garam masala, chilli powder and the ground cumin and coriander. Mix well, then add the chicken and lemon juice. Cover and leave to marinate for up to 24 hours.

Place the marinated chicken pieces in a single layer on a suitable rack for grilling. Brush the meat with a little vegetable oil and cook under a preheated hot grill for about 10 minutes, turning the chicken halfway through. To ensure the chicken is cooked, cut a piece in half to check. When done, cool thoroughly and chill.

Once cooled, thread the chicken onto cocktail sticks and garnish with finely chopped fresh coriander. Serve on a flat plate with a bowl of raita on the side.

For the mint raita

Peel and grate the cucumber, then squeeze out most of the moisture. Transfer to a bowl and mix thoroughly with all the other ingredients. Check the seasoning and adjust if necessary.

STICKY HONEY-GLAZED SAUSAGES

These small bites have been devoured at most of our wedding celebrations and corporate events up and down the county. We guarantee that you will have a gaggle of followers after they feast on these tasty morsels. Be sure to cook plenty as there are rarely any left over.

Preparation time: 10 minutes | Cooking time: 30-40 minutes | Makes 60

INGREDIENTS

120g hoisin sauce

120g runny honey

1 tablespoon grated fresh ginger

1kg thin Cumberland sausages
(natural skins are best)

Fresh parsley, chopped

METHOD

Preheat the oven to 180°c. Mix the hoisin sauce with the honey and ginger in a large bowl. Using a pair of scissors, cut the sausages into pieces about 2.5cm in length. If you're using chipolatas, cut each sausage into 3 bite-size pieces. Add the sausages to the bowl and turn them over very gently to coat each piece with the sauce.

Transfer the sausages and sauce to a roasting tray large enough for the sausages to be placed in a single layer. Cook in the oven for about 30 minutes, stirring gently halfway through. The sauce will thicken and become deliciously sticky.

Allow the sausages to cool in the sauce and then reheat as required. Serve on a warmed plate with a raised edge, garnished with some chopped parsley.

HINTS & TIPS

Use a shot glass to hold cocktail sticks and a small dish to collect used sticks for serving. The flavours in this recipe develop better if it's made the day before serving.

CONFETTI PUNCH & GARDEN HALL PUNCH

These recipes are both foolproof crowd-pleasers. The first is a sparkling, fruity
punch with a kick that's great for any celebration. For the non-alcoholic option, our
Food & Company Garden Hall Punch complements the Confetti Punch beautifully.

Preparation time: 10 minutes | Confetti Punch makes 30 glasses/Garden Hall Punch makes 20 glasses

INGREDIENTS

For Confetti Punch

1 bottle of white rum (70cl)

2 bottles of sparkling wine (150cl)

1 litre lemonade

1 litre sparkling white grape juice

½ litre orange juice

For Garden Hall Punch

1 litre orange juice

1 litre ginger beer

1 litre sparkling apple juice

To serve

Orange slices

Mint sprigs

Ice cubes

METHOD

For Confetti Punch

Chill all the punch ingredients. Before guests arrive, mix them together in
a large suitable container. To make serving the punch effortless, decant
into jugs.

For Garden Hall Punch

Chill all the ingredients. Combine the orange juice, ginger beer and
sparkling apple juice in large jugs then keep cold until serving.

To serve

For either punch, set your glasses on a tray and decorate each one with a
slice of orange and a sprig of mint. Shortly before serving, use an ice
bucket to add some ice cubes to the glasses and then fill with punch as
required. Ideally serve the punch in champagne flutes.

HINTS & TIPS

Leave the mint out of the glasses for Garden Hall Punch so that you know
who's having the alcoholic drink and who isn't.

CHRISTMAS ON A PLATE

These are recipes that we feel suit the festive period, not necessarily things you'd cook for Christmas lunch itself as there are so many traditional options for that already. It's a mixture of starters, mains, desserts, edible gifts and of course mince pies. For us, this time of year is all about family coming home for the holiday to be with loved ones, so the dishes here can mostly be prepared in advance and enjoyed when needed, allowing you to focus on the important things.

It's also a time for kindness, generosity and thinking about others. Taking gifts of homemade food is such a nice way to show someone you care about them, or to exchange friendly season's greetings with neighbours. We believe that a parcel of homemade mince pies or a jar of Tipsy Apricot Compôte (aside from being delicious) carries a lasting sentiment because you've made it with love.

When we were children, Christmas lunch had to be at 12 o' clock sharp so all the farming folk could get back to their jobs, such as milking the cows and doing up (feeding the stock). We love hosting the family Christmas day lunch on alternate years, but especially enjoy the year when it's not our turn to do the cooking! Everyone looks forward to the Christmas Wraps in this chapter, the recipe for which actually came from the family in California and is a perennial favourite.

Our Food & Company days come to a close at the end of November, then we finish the season with a hands-on workshop making Christmas door garlands. Hanging these up on our front doors always marks the end of another year for our business, and the start of Christmas for us all.

"No place like home"

CHRISTMAS WRAPS

Another recipe from over the pond. Catarina uses lavash flatbreads instead of the tortilla wraps for this family favourite. Great for any occasion and not just Christmas, this recipe is ideal for getting the children involved in making these delicious no-cook appetisers.

Preparation time: 10 minutes | Makes 36 pieces

INGREDIENTS

3 large soft wheat tortilla wraps

120g soft full-fat cream cheese

Rocket leaves

90g dried cranberries

Pinch of black pepper

9-12 slices of Parma ham or similar

METHOD

Lay out the tortilla wraps on the work surface, then divide and spread the cream cheese evenly over them. Sprinkle the rocket and cranberries over the cream cheese then gently press down to firm. Season with a little black pepper and then lay the slices of Parma ham over the rocket. Don't be afraid to be generous with the fillings.

Roll each tortilla up tightly and wrap in cling film, twisting the ends to keep the rolls tight. Chill the wraps until required. When ready to serve, remove the cling film and cut each wrap into 12 slender slices. Try to cut at an angle and then place them cut-side down onto a serving platter.

HINTS & TIPS

We recommend that you make these tasty morsels the day before and refrigerate until needed.

SMOKED SALMON CHOWDER

If you're ever lucky enough to receive a Christmas food hamper that includes smoked salmon, this recipe might be for you. Treat it as an indulgent starter or lunchtime dish for the Christmas holidays.

Preparation time: 10 minutes | Cooking time: 20 minutes | Serves 6

INGREDIENTS

500g potatoes, peeled

750ml vegetable or chicken stock

1 leek

Salt and black pepper, to taste

300ml double cream

200g sliced smoked salmon

Fresh chives, to garnish

METHOD

Dice the prepared potatoes into even cubes and place in a saucepan. Cover with the stock and bring to a gentle simmer. Cook for about 6 to 10 minutes or until the potatoes are almost tender. Clean and finely slice the leek before adding it to the saucepan along with a good grinding of black pepper, then bring back to a gentle simmer.

Pour the cream into a large jug and add a ladle of the hot soup to it. Stir until thoroughly blended before pouring the mixture back into the soup. Roll the slices of smoked salmon into sausages and use scissors to cut them into bite-size pieces. Place on top of the simmering soup, then reduce the heat and cook uncovered for a further 5 minutes. Stir gently, taking care not to break up the salmon. Check the seasoning and snip over some chives just before serving.

If serving the chowder immediately, ladle it into warmed bowls with chunks of Cheesy Soda Bread on the side. Otherwise, allow the chowder to cool, chill in the fridge, then reheat when required. For a classy dinner party, try serving this in coffee cans or teacups.

CHEESY SODA BREAD

A quick and easy recipe for a rustic loaf that you'll make again and again. It's all about that crunchy crust and soft interior. If you do happen to have any left over, it also makes great toast in the morning.

Preparation time: 10 minutes | Cooking time: 30 minutes | Makes 1 loaf

INGREDIENTS

120g wholemeal flour

120g plain flour

1 heaped teaspoon bicarbonate of soda

½ teaspoon salt

60g mature cheddar cheese, grated

3 tablespoons natural yoghurt

150ml milk

METHOD

Preheat the oven to 200°c. In a large bowl, mix together the flours, bicarbonate of soda, salt and cheese. Make a well in the centre of the mixture and add the yoghurt followed by the milk. Mix with a round-bladed knife to form a dough.

Turn the dough out onto a floured board and knead briefly, then form into a ball and flatten it to about 12cm in diameter. Mark the dough with a deep cross using a sharp knife, cutting about two thirds of the way through the loaf.

Place on a baking sheet and bake for about 30 minutes in the preheated oven until it sounds hollow when you tap it on the bottom. This soda bread is best eaten on the same day and served with our Smoked Salmon Chowder.

SPICED BEEF

This is a lovely recipe for any occasion, whether it's a festive gathering or a lunchtime sandwich. Get ahead and have the cooked beef in the fridge ready to go. Serve in thin slithers over the holidays for a tasty treat.

Preparation time: 5 minutes, plus up to 4 hours marinating | Cooking time: 6 minutes | Serves 6

INGREDIENTS

30g light brown sugar

1 teaspoon coarse sea salt

½ teaspoon ground star anise

1 tablespoon grated fresh ginger

1 clove of garlic, chopped

½ lemon, zested

1 teaspoon chilli jam

2 tablespoons light soy sauce

1 dessertspoon sesame oil

4 rump steaks (approx. 180g each)

Oil, for searing the beef

METHOD

Mix the sugar, salt, star anise, ginger, garlic, lemon zest, chilli jam, soy sauce and sesame oil together in a non-metallic shallow dish or container, just large enough to lay out the beef steaks in a single layer. Add the steaks and thoroughly coat with the marinade, then cover and place in the fridge or somewhere cool for at least 4 hours, turning them periodically.

Remove the steaks from the marinade and cook in a hot heavy-based frying pan or griddle for about 3 minutes on each side until medium. The timing can vary slightly depending on the thickness of the steaks. Cool the steaks, cover and chill until ready to serve.

To serve, cut the cold steaks into thin slithers and enjoy with Cranberry and Pear Relish on the side.

CRANBERRY AND PEAR RELISH

This seasonal relish is quick, easy to make, and delicious with all Christmas cold cuts. We love the noise of the cranberries popping as they cook and their bright jewelled colour. Their tartness is simply wonderful when paired with the warm spice of star anise.

Preparation time: 15 minutes | Cooking time: 20 minutes | Makes 600ml

INGREDIENTS

180g red onion

1 tablespoon vegetable oil

250g conference pears

300g cranberries, fresh or frozen

120g caster sugar

90ml white wine vinegar

1 clove of garlic, finely diced

1 tablespoon grated fresh ginger

1 teaspoon salt

½ teaspoon ground star anise

Pinch of ground white pepper

METHOD

Peel and finely dice the onions before frying them gently in the oil until soft. Peel, core and dice the pears, then add them to the onions along with all the remaining ingredients. Stir well and allow to slowly simmer.

After 15 to 20 minutes, when the cranberries have collapsed and the relish has thickened, remove the pan from the heat. Allow to cool before storing in an airtight container or suitable jar. Relishes in general have a shorter shelf-life, due to the small quantity of vinegar.

TURKEY FILO PIE

For Food & Co regulars, this recipe has become a classic to use up the leftover turkey on Boxing Day. The filo pastry makes this a quick and easy pie with a delicious combination of brown and white meat.

Preparation time: 30 minutes | Cooking time: 40 minutes | Serves 8

INGREDIENTS

45g butter

1 tablespoon vegetable oil

150g fresh spinach

1 medium leek, cleaned and sliced

60g long grain rice

150ml chicken or vegetable stock

125ml double cream

2 or more sprigs of thyme

Salt and black pepper, to taste

8 squares of filo pastry (approx. 25cm each)

360g cooked turkey, cut into bite-size pieces

90g Stilton cheese, crumbled

30g dried cranberries

METHOD

Heat 15g of the butter with the vegetable oil in a pan and add the spinach. Cook until wilted before draining well and squeezing out all the excess moisture. Set the spinach aside and melt the remaining butter in the pan. With the lid on, cook the leeks in the butter until they are soft.

Add the rice, coating it well with the buttery juices, then add the stock, cream and thyme. Cook gently until the liquid has almost evaporated and the rice is al dente. Remove and discard the woody stalk from the thyme and stir the spinach into the rice mixture. Season well with salt and pepper before allowing to cool.

Preheat the oven to 180°c and lightly grease a 24cm loose-bottomed flan tin. Using 6 squares of filo pastry, brush each sheet lightly with vegetable oil and line the tin. Lay the pastry at different angles so that the base is covered evenly while also ensuring that excess pastry hangs over the edge of the tin. Work briskly with the filo pastry to prevent it from drying out, halving the sheets if necessary. Be sure to set 2 sheets of pastry aside to cover the top of the pie.

Spread the cooked rice mixture over the pastry base and then cover with the cooked turkey pieces, crumbled Stilton, and dried cranberries. Cut the last 2 squares of pastry into quarters, brush lightly with oil and place over the turkey filling. Fold the overhanging pastry over the top of the pie to form a lid. Brush sparingly with oil. Bake on a middle shelf in the preheated oven for about 40 minutes and serve hot.

HINTS & TIPS

Best enjoyed straight from the oven.

Substitute the meat with roasted peppers and courgettes for a meat-free alternative.

Use leftover cranberry sauce instead of the dried cranberries if you like.

SLOW COOKED PORK
WITH FENNEL SEASONING

Deliciously different, this roast made with a cheaper cut is great to serve warm
with salads for an informal supper. A dollop of our Cranberry and Pear Relish
(see page 170) on the side works well with this recipe at Christmas, but apple sauce
is equally delicious at any other time.

Preparation time: 30 minutes | Cooking time: 6 hours | Serves 8-10

INGREDIENTS

2kg pork shoulder joint (no rind)

4 tablespoons fennel seeds

2 tablespoons coriander seeds

½ tablespoon coarse salt

½ tablespoon ground white pepper

1 tablespoon vegetable oil

2 medium onions, finely sliced

1 tablespoon soft dark brown sugar

2 tablespoons balsamic vinegar

1 tablespoon dried sage, or a small
bunch of fresh sage, chopped

Salt and black pepper, to taste

METHOD

To make the seasoning, dry roast the fennel and coriander seeds in a pan.
Once roasted, turn out onto a plate and allow to cool, then grind in a
pestle and mortar with the salt. Put the spice mix into a lidded jar, add the
white pepper and with the lid on, shake to mix well. Label the jar and use
as required.

Preheat the oven to 200°c and heat the vegetable oil in a pan. Add the
sliced onions and stir before covering with a lid. Cook on a medium heat
until soft. Add the sugar and balsamic vinegar and cook uncovered on
medium heat until all the liquid has evaporated. Add the sage and season
with salt and black pepper before allowing to cool.

Remove the string and open the shoulder joint, lay it flat on a board and
use a sharp knife to score the skin. Generously rub some of the fennel
spice mix over both sides of the pork. Spread the cold onion mixture over
the inside of one half and bring the joint back together to create an onion
pocket. Hold in place by tying tightly with string or cooking bands. Sprinkle
the scored skin with extra fennel spice and drizzle with oil.

Place the pork into a tight-fitting tray or casserole and cook uncovered for
about 30 minutes in the preheated oven. Reduce the temperature to
140°c, cover with a lid and cook very slowly for about 6 hours until tender.
Allow to rest, slice thinly and serve warm with salads.

HINTS & TIPS
This is a great recipe for anyone with an AGA cooker.
The remaining fennel spice can be used to season any pork dish.

CHRISTMAS BROCCOLI SALAD

This recipe, which Catarina shared with us, is the star of any buffet table. All the ingredients scream California, but the crisp green of the broccoli and the reds of the cranberries and apple remind us of Christmas. Oh, and by the way, it tastes fantastic.

Preparation time: 20 minutes | Serves 8

INGREDIENTS

½ red onion, finely diced

1 dessertspoon honey

1 dessertspoon olive oil

2 dessertspoons cider vinegar

1 large head of broccoli

1 large red apple, skin on and finely diced

3 tablespoons mayonnaise

Salt and black pepper, to taste

60g dried cranberries

60g walnuts

METHOD

In a large bowl, marinate the red onion in the honey, oil and cider vinegar and leave for at least an hour. This could also be left to marinate overnight.

Cut the broccoli florets into very small pieces, including some of the stem, and add to a pan of boiling salted water. Bring back to the boil, then immediately drain and refresh in cold water to prevent further cooking. Drain well and dry in a clean tea towel or use a salad spinner.

Add the chopped apples to the marinated onions and stir in the mayonnaise, then add a pinch of salt and pepper to taste. Just before serving, add the broccoli, cranberries and walnuts to the mixture. Turn out onto an attractive serving dish to make this salad really stand out as a seasonal winner.

HINTS & TIPS

Salad spinners are great for removing excess water from rinsed leaves before using and also blanched vegetables before freezing.

FESTIVE MERINGUE CAKE

This is a wonderfully light and delicious dessert which screams Christmas. The recipe below makes an impressive sky-high meringue. For busy people, the meringue shells can be made in advance and kept in an airtight container.

Preparation time: 25 minutes | Cooking time: 35-40 minutes | Serves 8

INGREDIENTS

For the meringue

60g pecans

60g dates

2 pieces of stem ginger in syrup

4 egg whites

240g caster sugar

½ teaspoon white wine vinegar

A few drops of vanilla extract

For the filling

300ml whipping cream

1 tablespoon stem ginger syrup

METHOD

Preheat the oven to 170°c. Line the base and sides of two 20 or 23cm loose-bottomed cake tins with baking paper, using a little bit of butter to stick the paper down if needed. Chop the pecans, dates and ginger.

In a large, clean and dry bowl, use an electric handheld whisk to whisk the egg whites until stiff, full of volume and dry looking. Gradually add the sugar while whisking and continue until thick and glossy. Add the white wine vinegar and vanilla extract, then whisk briefly until combined. Use a metal spoon to gently fold in the chopped pecans, dates and ginger.

Divide the mixture between the two lined tins, roughly smoothing the tops, and bake in the preheated oven for about 35 minutes. The meringues should have a crisp top and a soft and marshmallow-like texture inside.

Cool the meringues in the tins. When cold, remove with the papers still intact and store in an airtight container. Ensure the meringue is handled with care as the shell will be delicate. Don't worry if the meringue does break though, as it can be easily put back together.

To assemble the cake, remove the baking paper from one meringue and put it onto a flat serving plate. Whip the cream until it becomes stiff, then add the ginger syrup. Whisk briefly and then spread the filling over the meringue. Remove the paper from the second meringue, sandwich the two together and chill.

For the best results, fill the Festive Meringue Cake up to 3 hours before serving. Dust with icing sugar and enjoy it with brandied oranges or a winter compôte.

TIPSY APRICOT COMPÔTE

Thick plain yoghurt and granola with a spoonful of our tipsy apricots is one of the most heavenly breakfasts you can make. For a non-alcoholic version that's just as divine, use apple juice instead of brandy.

Preparation time: 12-24 hours | Cooking time: 25 minutes | Makes 2 jars

INGREDIENTS

250g dried soft apricots

1 mug of Earl Grey tea (enough to cover the apricots)

240g granulated sugar

10 cloves

2 cinnamon sticks

1 lemon

70ml brandy

METHOD

Cut the apricots into small pieces using kitchen scissors and place into a bowl. Cover with the freshly brewed tea and leave to soak overnight, or for up to 24 hours.

Drain the apricots, reserving 150ml of the tea. Pour this into a pan and add the sugar, cloves and cinnamon sticks. Use a potato peeler to pare the zest of the lemon and add it to the pan.

Heat the mixture gently until the sugar has fully dissolved. Add the drained apricots and bring to a simmer. Simmer without a lid for 15 minutes, then remove from the heat. Once the mixture is almost cold, stir in the brandy, then pour into clean, screw top jars and label.

SOZZLED SULTANAS

We love visiting the Jerez region of Spain for a glass or two of the local sherry. Pedro Ximénez grapes are dried in the sun before they're made into the most delicious, sticky sweet sherry that tastes just like Christmas pudding.

Preparation time: 1 week

INGREDIENTS

Sultanas

Pedro Ximénez Sherry

METHOD

Choose suitable jars with tight-fitting lids to store the sultanas in. Wash the jars in hot soapy water and sterilise before filling. Check the sultanas for stalks and remove them before putting in the clean jars. Fill the jars until they are about three quarters full and top up with the sherry.

Put the lids on and leave the jars sealed and stored in a cool place for at least 1 week to allow the fruit to plump up, but they will keep for up to 1 year. Remember to label and date each jar. Perfect served over vanilla ice cream.

CRANBERRY MINCEMEAT

There's no comparison between shop-bought and homemade mincemeat. Oozing with the flavours of dried fruit, nuts, warm spice and citrus, and enough brandy to warm the cockles of your heart, homemade wins hands down. This mincemeat can be used in a host of festive treats.

Preparation time: 15 minutes | Cooking time: 1 hour | Makes approx. 4 jars

INGREDIENTS

120g mixed peel

1 large cooking apple

2 oranges, zested and juiced

300g fresh cranberries

240g dried cranberries

240g raisins

240g sultanas

240g soft brown sugar

100g flaked almonds, roughly chopped

3 teaspoons mixed spice

½ teaspoon ground cinnamon

½ teaspoon freshly grated nutmeg

350ml brandy (not your best!)

100g vegetable suet, shredded

METHOD

Chop the mixed peel into a very small dice. Grate the cooking apple with the skin on, then put all the ingredients, excluding the brandy and vegetable suet, into a large non-metal bowl. Mix everything together, then cover and leave overnight to let the flavours develop.

Preheat the oven to 160°c and transfer the uncooked mincemeat into a large ovenproof casserole dish. Cover with a well-fitting lid and cook in the preheated oven for about 45 minutes, then stir and cook for a further 15 minutes.

Once cooked, remove the mincemeat from the oven and cool before adding the brandy and vegetable suet. Put into sterile, dated and labelled jars. The mincemeat will keep extremely well.

HINTS & TIPS

Frozen cranberries can be used as an alternative to the fresh cranberries in this recipe. Make this early in the season to allow the mincemeat time to mature before Christmas.

VIENNESE MINCE PIES

The legendary "Christmas Warm Up". Our first mince pie of the season is always at an early December drinks party held by friends. The delicate crisp pastry with a crumbly biscuit topping and homemade mincemeat lets us know that Christmas is here!

Preparation time: 35 minutes, plus 1 hour chilling | Cooking time: 20 minutes | Makes 24

INGREDIENTS

For the almond pastry

240g plain flour

90g caster sugar

90g ground almonds

Pinch of salt

180g butter

1 egg, beaten

For the Viennese topping

210g soft margarine

60g caster sugar

Few drops of vanilla extract

240g plain flour

METHOD

For the almond pastry

Sift the flour into a large bowl, add the sugar, almonds and salt and blend together. Cut the butter into small, even cubes and rub into the flour mixture until it resembles breadcrumbs. Add the beaten egg and bring the mixture together into a dough. Chill for at least 1 hour, but remember to remove the pastry from the fridge a little before it is required.

When the dough has chilled, divide the pastry in two. Freeze one half to keep for another time and roll out the other half on a lightly floured surface. Cut out discs using a 6.5cm fluted cutter and reroll the pastry offcuts until you have 24 discs in total.

For the Viennese topping

Use an electric mixer to cream the margarine, sugar and vanilla extract together until light and fluffy. Add the flour and beat well until it forms a soft and pliable mixture that you can pipe easily. Put the mixture into a piping bag fitted with a star-shaped nozzle and keep it somewhere warm.

To assemble the pies

Try our homemade cranberry mincemeat recipe (see page 182) or use your own favourite. Preheat the oven to 180°c and line two 12-hole patty tins with the almond pastry discs. Fill the pastry discs with mincemeat and pipe a circle of the soft Viennese topping around the outer edge of each mince pie. There should be a sufficient amount of mixture to pipe all 24.

Bake the mince pies in the preheated oven for about 20 minutes until lightly golden. Remove from the oven and leave them to cool in the tin for a few minutes before transferring to a cooling rack while they are still warm. Store the pies once they have cooled completely.

HINTS & TIPS

Delicious served warm or cold with a dollop of Cumberland Rum Butter (see page 22).
Decorate the plate of mince pies with a sprig of holly for a great seasonal look.

INGREDIENTS INDEX

Raspberry jam
Victoria Sandwich Cake 38

Red cabbage
Baked Red Cabbage with Chestnuts
& Venison Sausages 46

Red chilli
Thai Fishcakes with Cucumber Salad 116
Guacamole 130

Red onion
Spanish Meatballs with Tomato Sauce 114
Thai Fishcakes with Cucumber Salad 116
Guacamole 130
Mango Salsa 156
Cranberry and Pear Relish 170
Christmas Broccoli Salad 176

Rice
Almond Slice 18
Chicken Elizabeth 64
Paella 92
Spanish Meatballs with Tomato Sauce 114
Thai Green Chicken Curry 118
Bean Chilli 132
Turkey Filo Pie 172

Roasted peppers
Picnic Loaf 84
Quinoa & Feta Salad 136
Turkey Filo Pie 172

Rocket leaves
Picnic Loaf 84
Tuna Tartare 128
Roasted Sweet Potato Salad 136
Christmas Wraps 166

Rosemary
Penrith Peppered Lamb 50
Baked Cod with Fennel & Cannellini Beans 110

Rum
Dropped Scones & Cumberland Rum Butter 22
Cumberland Tarte Tatin 56
Rich Chocolate Slice 78
Confetti Punch & Garden Hall Punch 162
Viennese Mince Pies 184

S

Saffron
Paella 92
Baked Cod with Fennel & Cannellini Beans 110

Salami
Picnic Loaf 84
Pizza on the Grill 88

Salmon
Potted Solway Shrimps with Melba Toasts 42
Oven Baked Salmon with Onion Marmalade 70
Thai Fishcakes with Cucumber Salad 116
Smoked Salmon Chowder 168

Sausages
Baked Red Cabbage with Chestnuts
& Venison Sausages 46
Stuffed Cumberland Chicken
with Cream Sauce 48
Scotch Eggs 82
Cumberland Sausage Pinwheels 148
Sticky Honey-Glazed Sausages 160

Shallot
Coq au Vin 106
Thai Green Chicken Curry 118

Solway shrimps
Potted Solway Shrimps with Melba Toasts 42
Tiny Solway Shrimp Tarts 154

Soured cream
L.A. Fondue 126
Tuna Tartare 128
Beef Chilli 130
Bean Chilli 132

Spinach
Turkey Filo Pie 172

Spring onion
Greek Potato Salad 90
Thai Fishcakes with Cucumber Salad 116
L.A. Fondue 126
Tuna Tartare 128
Roasted Sweet Potato Salad 136
Quinoa & Feta Salad 136
Cheese & Chilli Scones 146

Stilton cheese
Turkey Filo Pie 172

Strawberries
Strawberries with Beaujolais
& Black Pepper Syrup 76
Cheese & Chilli Scones 146

Sultanas
Fruit Scones 26
Chicken Elizabeth 64
Roasted Sweet Potato Salad 136
Sozzled Sultanas 180
Cranberry Mincemeat 182

Swede
Turnip Gratin 52

Sweet potato
Roasted Sweet Potato Salad 136

T

Tahini
Oven Baked Salmon with Onion Marmalade 70

Tomato
Penrith Peppered Lamb 50
Chicken Elizabeth 64
Quiche Lorraine 66
Picnic Loaf 84
Pizza on the Grill 88
Baked Cod with Fennel & Cannellini Beans 110
Spanish Meatballs with Tomato Sauce 114
Mexican Baked Eggs 122
Tuna Tartare 128
Beef Chilli 130
Guacamole 130
Bean Chilli 132
Stuffed Aubergine Rolls with Tomato Sauce 134
Quinoa & Feta Salad 136
Mango Salsa 156
Chicken Tikka & Mint Raita 158

Treacle
Sticky Gingerbread 34
Food & Co's Grasmere Gingerbread 58

Tuna
Tuna Tartare 128

Turkey
Turkey Filo Pie 172

Turnip
Penrith Peppered Lamb 50
Turnip Gratin 52

V

Vanilla extract
Peanut Caramel Bars 32
Crème Brûlée 76
Baked Blueberry Cheesecake 140
Festive Meringue Cake 178
Viennese Mince Pies 184

Vegetable stock
Baked Cod with Fennel & Cannellini Beans 110
Bean Chilli 132
Turkey Filo Pie 172

Vegetable suet
Cranberry Mincemeat 182

Vermouth
Baked Cod with Fennel & Cannellini Beans 110
Two Ways with Crab Tarts 150

W

Walnuts
Parsnip & Walnut Tea Bread 30
Carrot & Coriander Muffins 124
Christmas Broccoli Salad 176

Watercress
Baked Chicken Gruyère 68

Whipping cream
Crème Brûlée 76
Festive Meringue Cake 178

White bread
Potted Solway Shrimps with Melba Toasts 42
Parsnip Bread & Butter Bake 62

Wine, red
Coq au Vin 106

Wine, white
Stuffed Cumberland Chicken
with Cream Sauce 48
Chicken Elizabeth 64
Paella 92
White Sangria 100
Chicken Liver Parfait 104
Baked Cod with Fennel & Cannellini Beans 110
Spanish Meatballs with Tomato Sauce 114
Thai Green Chicken Curry 118
Tuna Tartare 128

Y

Yeast
Pizza on the Grill 88

Yoghurt
Greek Potato Salad 90
Baked Peaches with Amaretto and Marsala 94
Honey Poached Pineapple
with Passionfruit Cream 96
Chicken Tikka & Mint Raita 158
Cheesy Soda Bread 168

It's grand ta be oot in t' oppen air
Oor Lakelan' haunts amang,
Whoar t' countryside's chock full o' charms
Few udder spots can bang.

Fer oor Lakelan' air's a tonic rare
'At maks a body thrive,
An' keeps yan weel an' prood ta feel
It's gud ta be alive.

Extract from Oot in T' Oppen Air - John Sewell. Thank you to the Lakeland Dialect Society. Illustration by Julie Asquith Coghlan.